L.

STEPPING-STONES

SYLVIA LEITH-ROSS

Stepping-Stones
Memoirs of Colonial Nigeria
1907–1960

Edited and with an Introduction by
MICHAEL CROWDER

PETER OWEN · LONDON AND BOSTON

ISBN 0 7206 0600 4

PETER OWEN PUBLISHERS
73 Kenway Road London SW5 0RE
and
99 Main Street Salem NH 03079

First published 1983
Text © Elizabeth Ganf 1983
Introduction, Notes and editorial matter © Michael Crowder 1983

Photoset and printed in Great Britain by
Photobooks (Bristol) Limited
Barton Manor St Philips Bristol

CONTENTS

ILLUSTRATIONS

PLATES

MAPS

EDITOR'S NOTE

Sylvia Leith-Ross had not finished editing her memoirs for publication before she died in February 1980. In fact, although she had completed a first draft by 1972 and had revised some of the chapters, it seems she gave the manuscript little attention thereafter. A member of Mrs Leith-Ross's family showed the manuscript to Beatrice Musgrave of Peter Owen Ltd with a view to publication. She was enthusiastic about its quality, but felt that it needed additional material to provide continuity and to illuminate some of the historical and personal background. At the suggestion of the family, she approached Professor Thurstan Shaw, a good friend of Sylvia Leith-Ross who wrote her obituary for *The Times*. He felt strongly that the manuscript deserved to be published and concurred with her assessment. Knowing of my own interest in the colonial period of Nigeria's history, he asked me whether I would take on the task of editing the manuscript for press. I found Sylvia Leith-Ross's memoirs a uniquely fascinating and beautifully written account of colonial Nigeria and readily agreed to take on the task.

Unfortunately, while the first five parts of the manuscript which was handed to me had been edited carefully by Sylvia Leith-Ross, she had only partially revised the last two parts, covering the years 1951 to 1960, which were, proportionate to the time-span they covered, much longer than the first five parts. They were also a mixture of two different versions, with some papers missing. Luckily, there was an undated handwritten note attached to them, stating:

> Parts 6 and 7 are a muddle of my original and revised versions. Both were sent separately to Rhodes House, but I no longer remember which is which. The original version, friends thought, was too sweeping. Both parts should be amalgamated, which would not be too difficult as the bulk of them stands.

The two versions were indeed in the Rhodes House Library, both complete. In preparing the present manuscript for press I have followed the suggestions for cutting or rewriting which Sylvia Leith-Ross had made in the margins of both versions. Thus this text is very much as she herself would have sent it to the publishers.

Sylvia Leith-Ross had given her manuscript the tentative title 'The Small Coins', taken from a passage in the *Tarikh es Soudan*. But it hardly reflected the content of her memoirs. She had, however, taken as one of her 'texts' a quotation from her famous book *African Women* in which she saw the British as 'stepping-stones' which the Nigerians quite consciously used on the path to freedom. This seemed a much more appropriate title for a book that covered Nigeria's history from the time of its subjection to colonial rule right up to its independence.

In editing Sylvia Leith-Ross's memoirs for press, I have tried to guard against interposing myself between the author and her readers, except insofar as explanation has been necessary for those not familiar with Nigeria and its history. In a very few cases I have inserted into her text short phrases to amplify or explain terms or institutions that would otherwise be unfamiliar to anyone but a specialist in the colonial period of Nigerian history. Where a longer explanation has been necessary I have prepared a section of Notes that can be found at the end of the book; with one exception, the footnotes are all Sylvia Leith-Ross's own. Otherwise the only additions I have felt essential are short linking passages describing the main changes that had taken place in Nigeria between each of her visits.

I have also provided in the Introduction a short biographical study of Mrs Leith-Ross that will help to set her Nigerian days in the perspective of her long life. It is reticent and brief because Sylvia Leith-Ross, as her relatives and friends will tell you, was herself very reticent, almost secretive in conversations about her life. But that is no matter, for she tells her story so well on paper, and I have preferred to let her speak for herself, albeit posthumously.

In the course of preparing *Stepping-Stones* for publication I have been greatly assisted by members of Sylvia Leith-Ross's family, who have supplied information or provided photographs. In particular I should like to thank William Ruxton, her nephew; Mrs Elizabeth Ganf, her niece and literary executor; Mary Paulo, her niece; and Andy Ganf, her great-nephew. I have also received assistance from Helen Callaway and Tony Kirk-Greene, Colin Hill, Thurstan Shaw, Bernard Fagg, Miss J. Dinnick-Parr, Michael Holloway, and Beatrice

Musgrave and Dan Franklin at Peter Owen. I am indebted to the librarians of Rhodes House and the London School of Economics, where a Visiting Fellowship in the Centre for International Studies has provided me with a quiet corner to complete this and several other projects.

MICHAEL CROWDER

Centre for International Studies
London School of Economics
and Political Science
June 1982

INTRODUCTION

Sylvia Leith-Ross first arrived in Northern Nigeria as a young bride in 1907, not long after Sir Frederick Lugard had finally brought that vast and diverse territory under British control. A year later she lost her husband from blackwater fever. But the land that caused his death did not thereby become her enemy. Rather she entered into a lifelong love affair with Nigeria and its peoples. Over the next sixty years she returned there again and again in different capacities. By the time of her last visit in 1968, at the age of eighty-five, she had travelled to most parts of the country and had lived for extended periods in all its major regions. After Nigeria gained her independence in 1960 she sat down to write a memoir of her various sojourns there. She worked on this from time to time until 1972 but never completed it for publication. It was only after her death in 1980 that it was read by some relatives and friends who realized that it made a unique contribution to the colonial history of Nigeria. And so it is now published.

We are fortunate to have this lively and penetrating account of the passage of a British protectorate from colonialism to independence. No Roman matron, as far as we know, joined her husband just after her countrymen had occupied Britain and then, despite his death from a chill while building roads across some East Anglian fen, returned again to the land she now loved though it had claimed her husband's life. Or if she did, she left no record of her travels in that far-off isle, or of her reaction to its peoples and to her fellow Romans who ruled them. If she had done, our understanding of the Roman occupation would have been the richer for it. In contrast, several wives of British administrators in Africa have left us accounts of their experiences. Mrs Larymore, for instance, travelled with her husband to Northern Nigeria just two years after Lugard had declared it a British Protectorate, and wrote *A Resident's Wife in Nigeria*.[1] This is a valuable source for the understanding of colonial rule in Nigeria in its formative phase, not because Mrs Larymore was the first British wife allowed to join her husband in that huge Protectorate, a great part of which still remained to be conquered, but because she provides insights into the colonial occupation that would have escaped her husband's eye.* But like all books of this genre, whether written by the wife of a colonial official, a woman missionary or woman anthropologist like Elenore Smith Bowen,[2] her account covers only a brief and territorially limited episode in the sixty-year-long history of British colonial rule in Nigeria. Together these books can tell us something of the attitudes of the British to their Nigerian subjects and the problems they faced, or thought they faced, as seen from the refreshing point of view of a woman in a male-dominated society. Yet, compared with the present memoir, they are as a series of snapshots of Nigeria's colonial past taken by different photographers, some with clearer focus than others.

★   ★   ★

Sylvia Leith-Ross was born on 30 September, 1883, at Pau in southern France, a country for which she retained a lifelong affection. Her father was Admiral Fitzherbert Ruxton, who, she liked to recall, also had Nigerian connections, for he had commanded the sloop *Pandora* which captured the last Portuguese slaver in the British Navy's prolonged campaign against the slave trade on the West Coast of Africa.[3] Her mother was Sylvia Howland Grinnell, an American whose parents came from leading Boston and New York families. After her father died, when she was only twelve years old, she was taken by her mother to Paris. There, despite their Protestant upbringing, she and her sister were entered in the Convent of the Sacred Heart. She had only spent a

---

* Could this observation on Keffi, a town whose ruler had killed the British Resident, Captain Moloney, and which had, as a result, been subjected to a punitive expedition by the British, have come from the pen of one of Lugard's political officers rather than from that of his wife?

> On the summit of a high hill, overlooking the town, was a circular wall, enclosing a solitary grave, the resting place of Captain Moloney, and, in the square, outside the Mosque, stood a tall white wooden cross, marking the spot where he died. All honour to those who placed it there – but that cross has always been a sorrow to me: close beside the wall of the Mosque, it could not fail to be an offence to a Mahommedan community, and, being on the way to the market, each man, woman and child who passed, must be reminded daily of the tragedy that ruined the prosperity of the town, and wrecked so many, innocent, humble homes.

year at the convent before her sister was asked to leave because 'some devil of obstinacy and indiscipline took hold of her and would not let her go'.[4]

Even though the young Sylvia 'tended to be the model pupil, and became the pride and example'[5] of her class, she too had to go. The year at the convent made a profound impression on her and, she maintained, opened for her 'the main doors into France' whose anguish in both the First and Second World Wars she was later to share, and recount so poignantly in her little book *Cocks in the Dawn*. No less of an impression was made on her by her 'finishing school' at Fontainebleau, where she gained 'that inestimable benefit of being able to see, not so much two sides of a question, but two nations' apprehensions of the same question.'[6] It was a facility she applied to advantage in her long association with another, and much more distant country, Nigeria, which she was to come to love as much as she admired and respected France.

If we except her father's earlier offshore connections with that country, this association had begun indirectly in 1898, when her brother, Upton Fitzherbert, ten years her senior and an army officer, was seconded to the Royal Niger Company. The chartered company's forces had recently conquered the Muslim Emirate of Ilorin, and Upton was posted there as Military Commandant and Senior Executive Officer of the Company. In 1900 he left to fight in the South African War where he was severely wounded. In 1901 he was seconded to the Colonial Office for service with Sir Frederick Lugard in the newly established British Protectorate of Northern Nigeria. There he befriended a young Canadian Lieutenant, Arthur Leith-Ross, who had been serving in the West African Frontier Force in Bornu Province,[7] and decided that he would make a fine husband for his sister Sylvia. A photographed miniature of her was sent for to entice him, and when Upton next went on home leave he took Leith-Ross with him. After meeting Sylvia he proposed marriage, was accepted, and application was made to Sir Frederick Lugard for permission for her to join him at Zungeru, the capital of the Protectorate, where Arthur Leith-Ross had recently been appointed Chief Transport Officer. Lugard gave his approval and in 1907 Sylvia Leith-Ross set off with Arthur to Zungeru, the third British wife allowed to join her husband in the Northern Protectorate.[8]

On 26 August, 1908, Arthur L., as she usually referred to him, died of blackwater fever. Not long before her own death in 1980, she was to recall that tragic event in greater detail than she does in her own memoirs. Talking with Charles Allen for his series of programmes for the BBC called 'Tales from the Dark Continent', she told him:

> My husband had had blackwater fever once before and had somehow survived, although he'd been completely alone. The second time it happened in Zungeru; one doesn't know why, it was just an infection, but at the time there was no known cure. He was at once taken to the small hospital and two doctors stayed with him day and night for two days, but he grew weaker and weaker and died within three days.
>
> Of course, death was accepted as part of the day's work, but he had been so much liked that the whole of his colleagues and even the black clerks and the transport boys were all shocked deeply and were, in a way, not so sorry for me as sorry for themselves in that they'd lost a friend and an example. Everybody was kindness itself to me but the only thing to do was for me to go home.[9]

Lugard too was to be shocked at the news and wrote later that Leith-Ross was 'an official of exceptional ability and initiative whose early death was a great loss to the country'.[10] Sylvia's love for Arthur L. never waned over the next seven decades she was to live without him. She only admitted one other love into her life, and that was the country she still barely knew and which had taken her husband from her.

She had to leave Zungeru after his death, there being no provision for the residence of white widows in that frontier town. But in 1910 she was permitted to return to stay with her brother, who was now Resident or British official in charge of Muri Province on the River Benue, to study the language of the Fulani, a nomadic cattle-keeping people to be found throughout northern Nigeria. She was made most welcome by Upton's generous and lively French wife, Geneviève, with whom she compiled *Practical West African Cookery* which they published locally for the use of other pioneer European women.[11]

She stayed twice with the Ruxtons, collecting materials for her *Fulani Grammar*. In between times she went to France to study under Professor Maurice Delafosse at the Ecole des Langues Orientales in Paris. There she took a room in a convent where the other ladies seemed to have an average age of seventy-two and were equipped with 'tongues like vipers and appetites like boa-constrictors'.[12] In *Cocks in the Dawn* she recalled the opening of one of Delafosse's lectures on the Fulani language (or Peul, as the French called it): '*Madame et Messieurs*, we will now study the laws of permutation as applied to the occlusive and constrictive consonants in the Fouta Djalon dialect of the Peul language. . . .'[13]

Sylvia Leith-Ross's *Fulani Grammar*[14] was not published until after the First World War, during which she had returned to France as a Red Cross volunteer. The *Grammar* – which, with characteristic modesty, she described as 'both intricate and superficial' – also included readings based on Fulani folk-tales and short English-Fulani, Fulani-English dictionaries.

From 1920–1925 Sylvia Leith-Ross worked as Secretary of the Tavistock Clinic, under its founder and Honorary Director, H. Crichton-Miller. He was later to write of her work: 'The difficulties with which she had to contend, the energy and determination with which she met these difficulties, are known only to myself and I can repeat what I have often said in public, that without her the Clinic would never have seen the light of day.'[15]

The circumstance of her return to Nigeria in 1925 was the appointment of her brother as Lieutenant-Governor of the Southern Provinces of Nigeria. Geneviève was unable to join him at the time so he invited Sylvia to act as his companion and hostess. While she stayed with him she met the Director of Education who offered her appointment as the first Lady Superintendent of Education in the country and as Secretary of the Board of Education for the Southern Provinces. In this capacity she was involved in the establishment of Queen's College, and later was asked to advise the Government of the Northern Provinces on the prospects for women's education in Ilorin.[16] In 1931, while based in Kano, where she was founding Headmistress of the Girls' Centre, she was invalided out of the Education Service.

Three years later, now aged fifty-one, she was given a Leverhulme Fellowship with Margaret Green to make studies of Ibo women in the aftermath of their riots that had so alarmed the colonial government in 1929, and had encouraged it to commission studies of the people whose social organization they had so clearly misunderstood or misinterpreted. These were the first studies to be made of the women who had been in the vanguard of the expression of Ibo discontent with the colonial administration. And significantly they were also being made by women. The results of Sylvia Leith-Ross's researches were published in 1939 as *African Women*, in many ways a pioneer work in the field of African studies. She recorded her experiences in a lighter vein in *African Conversation Piece*, still a delightful and perceptive entertainment today, and in which she recalled that when she set up house in Onitsha, 'all officials were most kind . . . though a little disapproving of white women going to live in native towns.'[17]

After her return to Britain she left for Perpignan where she helped to care for refugees from the Spanish Civil War. When the Second World War broke out, she was back in France again with the Red Cross and only left after the fall of France to the Germans, sharing the grief of the defeated French, for their country had in so many ways become her own.

Once again Sylvia Leith-Ross returned to Nigeria, this time to work in the Political and Economic Research Organization, the wartime intelligence organization known as 'PERO' for short. When she left in 1943, she little thought that she would ever see the country again. For she was now sixty years old, an age at which most colonial officials had long since retired.

Eight years later, with Nigeria now set firmly on the path to independence, she returned with what seemed to others a somewhat bizarre project of setting up a finishing school for girls in Onitsha, where she had been so happy as a Leverhulme Fellow. The school failed to appeal to the local élite and she gave the project scant attention in her memoirs and, indeed, good friends of hers as well as local British officials were very sceptical about the whole enterprise.[18] Despite the school's failure, she stayed on in Nigeria, a welcome guest in the houses of her many friends.

Then in 1956, Bernard Fagg, Curator of the Jos Museum, asked her whether she would like to make a collection of Nigerian pottery for him. And so Sylvia Leith-Ross, now over seventy, embarked on her last Nigerian career as an expert on pottery. To her indomitable energy over the next decade the fine exhibition of Nigerian pottery at the Nigerian Museum in Jos owes its existence. Her work was recognized in 1966 by the award of the MBE, while the research that underpins this collection is presented in what at the time seemed to be her last book, *Nigerian Pottery*, published in 1970.

In 1960, three months before Nigeria's independence, Sylvia Leith-Ross had paid her final farewell – as she thought – to the country with which she had been associated through most of its colonial experience. She was, however, to return to Nigeria eight more times, her last visit being in June 1968, sixty-one years after she first set foot in the country.* She did in fact visit West Africa once more the following year, staying for Christmas with her niece whose husband was working in Ghana. She returned to England in January 1970, now aged eighty-seven, and died a decade later, on 13 February, 1980, in the quiet of a convent. She was a remarkable woman by any standard; she was also a woman of great loyalty. As *The Times* obituary observed, 'the cross on Arthur Leith-Ross's grave at Zungeru bears the words "Faithful unto death"; his wife was faithful to her two loves for more than seventy years of her life.'

★   ★   ★

What kind of country was the Nigeria that Sylvia Leith-Ross came to in 1907? First of all, it was not one country, or rather colony, but two: the Protectorate of Northern Nigeria and the Colony and Protectorate of Southern Nigeria. The two British territories were separately administered, each with its own High Commissioner or Governor and its own civil service; and, as if to seal its identity, each had its separate issue of postage stamps. Northern Nigeria had formally been declared a British Protectorate on 1 January, 1900, when the Union Jack was raised at Lokoja at the confluence of the Benue and the Niger Rivers. Three years earlier the Muslim Emirates of Ilorin and Bida had been conquered for Britain by the Royal Niger Company, which had been given a Charter by the British Crown to administer lands south and north of the confluence in its name. In 1900 the Charter was withdrawn because of the Company's incapacity to deal with the problems involved in governing huge tracts of Nigerian territory, the unpopularity of its government among those subjected to it, and, most important of all, the risk of conflict with the French who were moving into lands to which it laid claim. Its territories – occupied or claimed – were then divided between the new Protectorate of Northern Nigeria and the Protectorate of Southern Nigeria which was simultaneously created from the southern part of these territories and the British Niger Coast Protectorate. In 1906 the Protectorate of Southern Nigeria was ex-

* It was during one of these visits that I had my one brief meeting with her, in Lagos. I still remember vividly my wonder that someone nearing her eightieth birthday should be undertaking so arduous a task as collecting pots from villages whose only access was often by back-breaking dirt roads.

tended to include the Lagos Colony and Protectorate. Meanwhile the Royal Niger Company lost its regal adjective and continued to trade in Nigeria as the largest single British commercial company with stores or 'canteens', as they were known, in every small town in Nigeria, selling pots and pans, sugar and soap, matchets and hoes, while their agents bought up the cotton, palm-oil or groundnuts produced by their customers. In 1920 W. H. Lever acquired the Company, and in 1929 it was amalgamated with other companies he owned and renamed the United Africa Company.

Though the Northern and Southern Protectorates were amalgamated in 1914 by Sir Frederick Lugard, the conquistador and High Commissioner of Northern Nigera from 1900–1906, they retained their separate personality until independence in 1960 and, alas for the stability of the new nation, for some time thereafter. In part the blame for this must be laid at the feet of the British, for the amalgamation was rather a federation in which the two constituent territories were allowed to go very much their own way. From the start there developed an unhealthy rivalry between the British administrators of the two protectorates and this continued after their amalgamation. It was said at the time of independence that if all the Nigerians had been removed from Nigeria then the British administrators of the North would have gone to war with those of the South.

Nevertheless, there were major basic differences between the two protectorates which British policy after amalgamation served to exacerbate rather than minimize.

The peoples of Southern Nigeria had been open to European influences much longer than those of the North. European traders had been active along the coast from as long ago as the end of the fifteenth century, while Lagos was taken by the British in 1861. Christian missionaries had begun the penetration of both the south-west and south-east of Nigeria in the early nineteenth century. The influence of Islam in the area was small and limited to certain Yoruba states and the areas north of Benin. By contrast, in the North Islam was the dominant religion, being the official faith of the huge Sokoto Caliphate which, together with Muslim Borno, made up most of Northern Nigeria. The rest of the territory comprised pockets of peoples who had resisted the forces of these two great states and the majority of these adhered to their own religions, which in British administrative parlance were designated 'pagan'. Hausa, the language of the major ethnic group of Northern Nigeria, had also become a language of trade and had de-

veloped into a lingua franca over much of what was to become
Northern Nigeria. In the South, no African lingua franca developed,
partly because there were two major ethnic groups rather than one – the
Yoruba in the south-west and the Ibo in the south-east – and partly because the extension of mission education spread the knowledge of the
English language which, with the pidgin developed by Africans trading with Europeans, served as a lingua franca.

When Sylvia Leith-Ross arrived in the Northern Protectorate,
Zungeru, its capital, had only just been effectively conquered. Sokoto
fell to the British only in 1903, and in 1906 there was a major rising in a
town nearby that seemed as if it might place the future of the British
administration in jeopardy. Led by a Malam Isa, a Muslim funda-
mentalist who proclaimed himself to be the prophet Jesus, it would
have spelt disaster for the British if it had had the support of the Sultan
of Sokoto. He came out in support of the British, though some of the
other traditional rulers wavered in their 'loyalty'.

In 1907 many of the so-called 'pagan' areas had not yet been subdued, while in other areas chiefs still continued to conduct slave raids,
suppression of which Lugard had used as one of the justifications for
the conquest. So even in 1907 the military were frequently sent on expeditions to subjugate a particular area where British authority was not
already established, or to mete out punishment to those who continued
to raid for slaves or refused to pay taxes. These expeditions were the
'scraps' that Sylvia Leith-Ross refers to in the early part of her
memoirs.

In 1907 the British administration in the North was, however, by
and large secure. The pattern of administration had been laid down.
The High Commissioner at Zungeru presided over a number of
provinces, each administered by a Resident, and by a number of
Assistant Residents, though on occasions a province nearly the size of
Portugal might be administered by a Resident and a single Assistant
Resident. In 1907 the European civil and military administration of
Northern Nigeria, which was some 200,000 square miles in area, numbered less than five hundred. Later on the Assistant Residents were renamed Senior District Officer, District Officer or Assistant District
Officer according to their experience. These DOs, as they were called,
supervised the work of the Native Administrations which might con-
sist of a traditional ruler, usually an emir, as sole Native Authority, or
else a traditional ruler with his council. The system of ruling through
the native chiefs was known as Indirect Rule and was the logical solu-

tion to the problem of the paucity of the British officials available to Lugard. Over the years a whole doctrine, associated with Lugard's name, grew up around the theme of Indirect Rule as it was practised in Northern Nigeria and was applied in most parts of Britain's African empire. It centred mainly on the principle of the Native Authority having the right to tax in its own name, but remitting a fixed proportion to the central colonial government; retaining formal judicial powers though certain classes of judgement were subject to review by the Administrative Officer; and being responsible for the administration of basic services for the people, such as markets, road-building, etc. In the large emirates like Kano, the Native Authorities administered huge budgets by the standards of the day, and were even to employ British officials directly.

The system of Indirect Rule was exported to the South by Lugard when he amalgamated the two Nigerias, but it met with resistance, particularly in Yorubaland where the powers of direct personal taxation now given to the traditional rulers were quite alien and were bitterly resented. In the East the application, or rather misapplication, of Lugardian Indirect Rule was to result in widespread riots by the women and it was in the aftermath of these that Mrs Leith-Ross was to make her study of African women among the Ibo.

When Sylvia Leith-Ross first arrived in Zungeru there were few roads in the Northern Protectorate, only a short length of railway line, and almost no exports. Groundnuts and cotton, which were to be the staple exports of later years, had not yet been developed as cash crops. The one major item of export was the tin mined on the Jos Plateau; the cool climate there made it ideal for European residence, but its exclusively 'pagan' population made it seem like a separate world.

To survive, the Northern Nigerian administration had to be given grants-in-aid by the British Government, contravening the Colonial Office philosophy that colonies should pay for themselves. One of the reasons for the amalgamation of Northern with Southern Nigeria was to be that the northern deficit would be easily covered by the healthy southern surplus, some of which came from duties on goods exported from Northern Nigeria but levied on the ports of the South.

The Northern Nigeria of 1907 had very much a frontier aspect. The British who came to serve there thought of themselves as pioneers, often taking responsibility for lands and peoples they knew nothing about. They were subject to diseases for which there was as yet no known cure, in particular blackwater fever, yellow fever, cerebral-spinal meningitis and river-blindness, as well as the more common dangers of dysentery and malaria. They established themselves in small settlements outside the headquarters town of the area they were to administer and called these 'stations' or 'cantonments'. Since the early Residents were in the main the military officers who had helped in the conquest, military terminology often crept into the administrative vocabulary. Thus the transport depot was often referred to as the 'transport lines'. And they began to place their imprint on Nigeria in the form of European-style bungalows and furniture built and constructed by the Public Works Department, known not always affectionately as the 'PWD'. The Political Officers had high standards of honesty and integrity, though they often lacked imagination. They administered minute budgets or 'votes' parsimoniously, knowing that the High Commissioner himself might query the smallest item of expenditure.

In those early years they were usually men without women, for not until the 'thirties did British wives begin to join their husbands as a matter of course. Often they lived on their own, alongside a remote Nigerian community, not seeing a fellow countryman for months on end. For the most part their stations were in hot, dry savannah, and their only means of transport the horse. Some succumbed to the boredom and isolation by drinking too much, but a remarkable number survived. The novels of Joyce Cary, who served as a District Officer in Nigeria from 1914 to 1919, and more especially his diaries (now in the Bodleian Library at Oxford), give some idea of the way District Officers sought to cope with this huge and alien world.[19]

There could be no single prescription for administering Northern Nigeria: the country comprised a great variety of peoples speaking a great variety of languages and with very different customs. So each station was a new challenge. Only in the 'Holy North', as it was known in local administrative parlance, was there some similarity between the emirates. The *jihad* or Holy War of Uthman dan Fodio, which lasted from 1804–1816, had brought the several Hausa states and many other parts of the Protectorate under the administration of the Caliph at Sokoto and had imposed some uniformity over the area. The constituent emirates were all supposed to be governed according to the *sharia*, or Muslim law. In reality, tradition intervened, but there was a common core of practice among the emirates. It was in the 'pagan' southern parts of the Northern Protectorate, particularly among the Tiv and Idoma, where Islam had never penetrated and where there was not the cool climate of Jos Plateau to compensate, that the problems of administration were seen as the most difficult. To be posted to Tiv was tantamount to being sent to a punishment station, while a posting to the Holy North was a prelude to promotion.

The Holy North was kept intact by a jealous British raj who would only permit Christian missionaries to proselytize in the emirates with the permission of the emirs themselves. Since, as Muslims, few were prepared to entertain a Christian missionary presence, and since the missionaries were the main instrument for the introduction of Western education, the North fell far behind the South in the field of Western learning. It did of course have its own scholarly tradition and the leaders of the *jihad* had been men of great erudition. Missionaries were allowed to operate freely only in the 'pagan' areas or what came to be known as the Middle Belt, that slice of central Nigeria that never came under the control of Borno or Sokoto, and even there they did so under the watchful and not always sympathetic eye of the administration.

As a result of this policy Islam consolidated its hold in those areas which had fallen under these two states and Christianity made great headway in the areas they had not succeeded in conquering. The Hausa, Kanuri, and the settled Fulani from among whom the leaders of the *jihad* had come, were almost exclusively Muslim. Among the other groups, Islam and Christianity vied for supremacy during the colonial regime.

All this can be written with the advantage of hindsight. At the time Sylvia Leith-Ross arrived in the North, the administration was only just setting about establishing its own Domesday Book for Northern Nigeria by means of the assessment reports the Assistant Residents or, later, District Officers had to make of the areas under their control. And it was with a sense of wonder that many of them surveyed this huge land.

★　　　★　　　★

Sylvia Leith-Ross too never lost her sense of wonder during all the years of her long involvement with Nigeria. But, although she was of the colonial class both by birth and marriage, she could distance herself sufficiently from her background to question the *modus operandi* of British colonial rule even if she did not challenge its fundamental assumptions. It is this combination of deep affection and wonder with critical detachment that makes her memoir so remarkable. She did not attempt to rewrite or recast her earlier impressions of Nigeria over the half century after she first arrived there to suit the changed perspectives of the 'seventies. She is quite frank in her criticisms of both Africans and Europeans, and perceives the changes in her own attitudes and in attitudes in Nigeria during the intervals between her visits.

At times some of her strictures on Nigeria's readiness for self-government may seem somewhat severe, but they provide, I believe, a truer picture for the historian of what British administrators felt about the timing of independence than the bland reminiscences of many colonial administrators who, in the context of the climate of opinion of the 1980s, are somehow ashamed to admit to having had these doubts.

Certainly her account of current attitudes reflects what those who, like myself, were witness to the last years of colonial rule in Nigeria remember them to have been. So Mrs Leith-Ross, who did not alter her memoirs to represent herself retrospectively in a more 'liberal' light, has left us an historically more valuable memoir than those who are more concerned with posterity's verdict on themselves. The truth is that the majority of the administrative class in the 1950s had serious reservations about the future of Nigeria without them, as Mrs Leith-Ross makes clear. She does not mask the fact that she shared their fears, nor that these fears in her opinion arose in many cases from the failings of the administrative class. She recaptures the agonizing that went on at the European cocktail parties, expresses frankly doubts that white men sought to conceal. But she is equally frank about her reservations concerning the British record in Africa. In *African Conversation Piece*, published just before the end of the Second World War, which she recognized had so dramatically changed Nigeria, she asked: 'Beautiful, immense, beloved and uncomprehended Africa. What have we brought you? What have we done to you? Change of some kind would have come anyhow, but have we, we white men, done the best that this change should be good?'[20]

Sylvia Leith-Ross's ability to see both sides and her unwavering search for truth – she points out that 'facts and thought change imperceptibly in remembrance' but guards against such changes closely – make her memoir an invaluable source for the future historian of colonial rule in Nigeria. For Nigerian historians in particular it provides an insight into the colonial class that does not attempt to gloss over the doubts she as well as many of her fellow members of that class had about the transfer of power. But it is more than just a source: it is a delightful account for anyone who is caught up in the current *nostalgie de l'Empire* and, above all, it is the unique testimony of an extraordinary woman's experiences in the country she made her second home and to which she was compelled to return again and again for over half a century.

NOTES

1 Constance Larymore, *A Resident's Wife in Nigeria*, London, 1908, p. 53.

2 Elenore Smith Bowen, *Return to Laughter*, London, 1954. Other books written by wives during or about the colonial period include Olive Macleod's *Chiefs and Cities of Central Africa*, Isabelle Vischer's *Croquis et souvenirs de la Nigérie du Nord*, Mrs Horace Tremlett's *With the Tin Gods*, Mary F. Smith's *Baba of Karo*, Laura Boyle's *Diary of a Colonial Officer's Wife*, Decima Moore's *We Two in West Africa*, Elner Russell's *Bush Life in Nigeria* and Rosemary Hollis's *A Scorpion for Tea*.

3 See the obituary of Sylvia Leith-Ross published in *The Times*, 22 February, 1980.

4 Sylvia Leith-Ross, *Cocks in the Dawn*, London, 1944, p. 12.

5 Ibid.

6 Ibid., p. 17.

7 Now spelt Borno. I have used the contemporary spellings of names where they refer to colonial administrative divisions.

8 In principle Lugard favoured the idea of wives joining husbands. But as he pointed out in a Memorandum on the 'Presence of Officers' Wives in the Protectorate' sent to the Colonial Office in 1904, it was impossible for any officers to take them out except those civil officers permanently stationed at Zungeru or Lokoja. 'If these officers are allowed, and encouraged by the building of suitable quarters, to take their wives out,' H. A. Butler of the Colonial Office minuted to his immediate superior, Antrobus, 'something would no doubt be added to the amenities of life at the two stations, and the service of the officers concerned would possibly be the more cheerfully and effectively rendered' (Butler to Antrobus, 22 September, 1904, minute on Lugard's despatch of 2 July, 1904, to the Secretary of State for Colonies, PRO/CO 446/39).

9 Published in Charles Allen (ed.), *Tales from the Dark Continent: Images of British Colonial Africa in the Twentieth Century*, London, 1979, p. 31.

10 Lord Lugard in his Foreword to Sylvia Leith-Ross, *African Women*, London, 1939, p. 5.

11 I have not been able to locate a copy of this book, first published in Zungeru in 1908, with a second edition published in Ibi in 1910. At some stage it seems to have been renamed *West African Cookery Book*, the title Sylvia Leith-Ross uses in her memoirs and by which it was known to many a newly-arrived Political Officer. Sir Bryan Sharwood Smith, who was Lieutenant-Governor of the Northern Region from 1952-57, the years in which self-government and independence were being negotiated, recalled in his own memoirs, *But Always as Friends*, that it made 'a

permanent contribution to the well-being of young bachelors new to the country, its greatest virtue being its emphasis on the value of local foods, normally scorned by Nigerian cooks who preferred using a tin-opener to marketing.'

12 *Cocks in the Dawn*, p. 21.

13 Ibid., p. 26.

14 Sylvia Leith-Ross, *Fulani Grammar*, published by the Government of Nigeria and sold by The Secretariat Stationery Store, Lagos, n.d.

15 Testimonial dated 21 February, 1933.

16 Memorandum on 'Female Education', Ilorin, submitted by Mrs Leith-Ross, Lady Superintendent of Education. Available in Rhodes House Library, Oxford, Sylvia Leith-Ross Papers.

17 Sylvia Leith-Ross, *African Conversation Piece*, London, 1944, p. 14.

18 See Colin Hill's account in the note on pp. 183–4.

19 For a study of the British political class in Northern Nigeria see Robert Heussler, *The British in Northern Nigeria*, London, 1968. See also M. M. Mahood, *Joyce Cary's Africa*, London, 1964, pp. 33–62 and my *Revolt in Bussa: A Study in British 'Native Administration' in Nigerian Borgu, 1902–1935*, London, 1973, for details of Joyce Cary's career in Borgu.

20 *African Conversation Piece*, p. 31.

They tolerate us because they need us. They do not look upon us resentfully as conquerors but complacently as stepping-stones. What will happen when they can, or think they can, mount alone and have no further use for the stepping-stones, no one can tell.

SYLVIA LEITH-ROSS
African Women, 1939

PREFACE

'What was it like in the old days?' is a question I have often been asked since, by chance, I am one of the few to have seen the beginning of British Government in Northern Nigeria, the middle period in Southern Nigeria, and the end in Northern Nigeria once more.

Many added: 'You should write it all down, before it is forgotten!' Yet my memories seemed too narrow, too concerned with individuals and details to be of interest. Then I remembered the noble words of Es Sa'di, the historian of Timbuctoo: 'Now am I present at the ruin of the Science of History, and I watch it vanish, both the gold and the small coins of it . . . therefore I will resolve to write down, myself, all that I know.' The gold is in safe hands. Of the many small coins I have hoarded, some may have significance only for myself, some are perhaps counterfeit, others may have less value than before, yet they represent the small exchange of daily life, of individual opinions, of what was said among the people; and they may give an inkling of the imponderable adjustments involved in a country's change of status and of the attitudes of the lesser people to that change.

I have wished to record only what I, myself, in my small but varied circle, have seen and heard, taking it for granted that little background is needed now that Nigeria has become so widely known.

Though I have seldom made any reference to the commercial community, it is not because I do not realize its immense importance to the development of Nigeria: it just so happens, insofar as Europeans are concerned, that I moved mostly among Government and Missionary people and knew their talk and outlook.

Among Africans, I have moved in many circles throughout these long years, grateful for their acceptance, honoured by their confidence. If I seem to regret, as we all do at times, the simplicities of the past, it is only because I wish so earnestly that the virtues of that past may be carried on into a still better and wider future.

S.L.-R.
1972

PART I: 1907–1908

As for power, we never even thought about it.

L. E. Jones,
An Edwardian Youth

It was in 1900 that Sir Frederick Lugard[1] as High Commissioner took over Northern Nigeria from the Royal Niger Company. It was in 1907 that, newly married, I came out with my husband to Zungeru, the latest capital of the Protectorate.

My husband's career had already been a vivid one. A Scots Canadian, he was at the Royal Kingston Military College in Ontario when the South African war broke out. He asked permission to join a Canadian contingent going overseas. His request was refused and as, poor and without influence, he saw no hope of gaining the Field Marshal's baton of which he dreamed except on active service, he deserted, found a troopship at Quebec and stowed himself away. Three days out at sea he reported to the Officer Commanding and, well up in *Regulations*, suggested that he should be shot. Instead, he received a sergeant's stripes and, after the British victory over the Boers at Paardeberg in 1900, was given a commission in the Lancashire Fusiliers. Later, when volunteers were asked for from South Africa for the Ashanti expedition under Sir James Willcox,[2] he applied at once, was accepted and left for Cape Town. Unfortunately the direct boat for the Gold Coast had already sailed, and owing to a series of delays he and his companion arrived too late, the Ashanti War was over. But almost immediately it was made known there was a grave shortage of officers in Northern Nigeria, where trouble was anticipated, and my husband was seconded from his regiment to serve with the West African Frontier Force. He was on the arduous Aro Expedition;[3] several others followed, forgotten 'shows' which at the time must have seemed so important, and often were, seen in the context of the then existing circumstances. After a spell in Bornu with the WAFF, Sir Frederick Lugard appointed him as first Chief

Transport Officer, and thus it was that our year of married life
was spent at Zungeru.

Alas, there was not so very much difference between the headquarters Zungeru of 1907 and the desolate Zungeru of today.
The bricks of the Government offices in Aiki Square lay neatly
one on top of the other instead of scattered in the dusty grass; the
roads ran straight and cleared instead of being half-lost tracks
across the sand and laterite. There may have been a bougain-
villaea or a couple of cannas instead of elephant grass and tough
stunted scrub, but the arid stony hills were the same, the relent-
less glare, the motionless heat, the glowering yellow sky over the
grey featureless scene. It was said the site had been chosen
partly for strategic reasons as it was centrally situated away from
any large native town and in a sparsely populated area. Far from
marsh or forest, it was considered healthy; the Kaduna River, on
whose banks it stood, had good water (and good fishing) and the
district was free from tsetse. It was into these austere surroundings that the long journey out from England took us.

How long it was, I cannot remember. There were weekly
Elder Dempster mailboat sailings then. The boat train to Liverpool, the jovial tones of the Old Coasters, the more subdued
ones of the newcomers, that strange band from a Boys' Home
which played semi-martial tunes with mournful zest, the
anxious faces peering round corners or trying to glimpse the
names on the mounds of luggage – envoys perhaps from Messrs
Way or from Griffiths, McAlister, seeking to get their accounts
paid up before their customer sailed for the White Man's Grave;
the extraordinary accoutrements that came on board, the sun-
helmets and guns, camp-chairs and saddles, chop boxes and
Lord's lamps,[4] camp-beds and green-lined umbrellas and, in
our case, an elegant, highly varnished, high-sprung dogcart –
all this gave a sense of gay adventure to those who were going, of
perils and heartbreaks to those who were left behind.

Today, watching a plane-load of mothers and babies and
schoolchildren, prams and feeding bottles and teddy bears, take
off for Kano or Lagos, it is almost impossible to recall that the
Coast had such a dark reputation only fifty years ago. It was deserved. By chance, I have this moment picked up *Niger Dawn* by

one of the early CMS [Church Missionary Society] missionaries, Frances Hinsley.[5] Reading only two and a half pages, I
find she already mentions the death of six missionaries. Every
expedition from Mungo Park onwards had lost all or a great part
of its members. Even at the time of which I write, and in spite
of the fact that the men who came out were young and
physically fit, official statistics stated that one in five of the
European population either died or was invalided home every
year.

My own family, used to foreign parts, paid little attention, but
to the general public the Coast was an evil legend. Either you
died of fever or of drink, went mad through loneliness or, worst
of all, went native. Yet, since all those who went there were presumably adventurers or remittance men, perhaps it did not
matter so much after all. When that absurd play *White Cargo*
was put on the stage in the early 1920s, with its forlorn white
men, the whisky bottles, the shameless half-caste girl, the
audience shrugged its shoulders and said: 'What else could you
expect?' Maybe only a few mothers went home and wept, thinking of their dear boys amid such perils. Yet their English
susceptibilities had been partly spared. The white father of the
half-caste girl was a Colonel, but it was expressly stated that he
was a French Colonel. . . .

Few wives accompanied their husbands in 1907; indeed an
official could not take his wife to Northern Nigeria without the
High Commissioner's express permission. No white woman
would have dreamt of having a baby in such a deadly climate and
there was not a white child in the whole country. It was not only
the climate which was considered so dangerous – after all, as a
people we were fairly inured to tropical conditions, and West
Africa had not the monopoly of malaria or dysentery or sun-
stroke or even of poisoned arrows. It was rather the absence of
all comfort, especially in the hardly settled North, the lack of
immediate help, the isolation of many of the officials and the
slowness of communications. By the time the runner had
reached the doctor, and the doctor, on foot, on horseback or by
canoe, had reached his patient, there was little hope left. Even if
the patient were still alive, how get him down to the Coast and
the chance of a homeward-bound ship or, alternatively, where
nurse him back to health in the country itself? There were no hill

stations as in India and no escape from the heat and the dust and the monotonous food.

Yet neither actual knowledge nor gloomy conjectures deterred those who felt what has been rather too romantically named 'the call of the Coast'. On this my first voyage I was too young to wonder as to motives. I probably took it for granted that, like myself, my companions thought it all a fine adventure, a compound of Rudyard Kipling and *Blackwood's* and *The Boys' Own Annual*, with deep underneath an unspoken belief that it was up to us, the British – since by a series of haphazard circumstances of which we usually knew very little, Nigeria seemed to have come into our care – to see fair play, to 'drive the road and bridge the ford', and to make sure 'to each his own that he shall reap where he has sown'. It was as simple – perhaps as childish – as all that. Certainly I do not think that any of these men thought of themselves as imperialists or colonialists or as any of the many-syllabled terms with which they are now adorned. Of course the aims of those in high places would have been more subtle, far-reaching, possibly self-seeking; but even now, looking back with a more adult judgement than I had then, I can see no sinister shadow on those bland faces, no innocent blood upon their hands. At the same time, I realize now that the simple fine adventure motive was not the only one. My husband went to Nigeria because pride made him ambitious and humility made him wish to serve. My brother, Major Upton Fitzherbert Ruxton, went because life with his regiment in England was dull. He was at first intellectually, then humanly and devotedly, interested in the future of the black peoples. Another man on that first trip went perhaps to escape from himself, having all the faults of his virtues. He died before the year was out. Another went because of some inner drive, a self-abandonment for others which set him apart. He also died. There was a young soldier, cheerful and guileless, who went for the shooting and the fishing and the chance of a scrap. 'Can't let these fellows go on slave raiding, can we?' He also wanted to see fair play, to tidy up, to make the roads safe. He died too.

The journey of approximately twenty-one days was uneventful, though less monotonous than it is today as ships sailed much nearer the coast and called at more ports. The usual run was: the Islands – the Catalina Hotel at Las Palmas was already open (can any old West Coaster smell a leaf of scented geranium without remembering its lovely garden and its large cool rooms, last sight of elegance on the outward journey, first touch of Europe on the homeward?) – then came Freetown, Monrovia, Axim, Sekondi, Cape Coast Castle, Accra, Lagos, Burutu. The Elder Dempster boats were small, the cabins tiny, fan-less and oven-hot. We washed in rust-yellow water poured daily into a rusty tank. Of the dining-saloon, I remember little save the pallid faces of the stewards, the many times we were served with Lancashire hot-pot, and the care with which those going to Northern Nigeria were segregated from those going to Southern Nigeria. It was not till 1914 that the two Nigerias were amalgamated under one Governor-General. Till then, no colour bar could be as strong as the intangible wall which stood between the Protectorate of Northern Nigeria and the Colony and Protectorate of Southern Nigeria. Even on the neutral ground of shipboard, no purser would have dreamt of asking a Northerner and a Southerner to share the same cabin, nor would a chief steward have ventured to seat them at the same table. Though no one could give me a rational explanation of this enmity, I immediately shared the prejudice, saw all Southern officials as fat and white and flabby, while in the North they were lean and lank and brown; knew they began drinks at 6 pm while we waited till 6.30 pm, and believed the grim tale that they travelled *carried in a hammock* while we galloped on horses or climbed arduous hills on our own feet.

Whatever the reasons may have been, it was with a slightly disdainful pity that we watched the passengers for Lagos and its hinterland being lowered one by one in a swaying mammy chair[6] into the heaving surf boat which alone could get across the bar. The company left on board the Elder Dempster was very small. The other two wives had been dropped, one at Freetown, one at Axim – I have often wondered what became of her, young and pretty in an empty-headed, golden-haired way. She had a new revolver ('in case the natives attack us') and a new hat ('my husband wrote I would be asked out a lot'). Axim, low and bare and brown, burned in the sun. The husband, agent for a European firm, came on board to meet her, but she had only eyes of dismay for that lonely scatter of buildings on that cruel shore. As, already tearful, she was swung down in the mammy chair, the new hat blew into the sea. I still see her poor little crumpled face against the immensity of sea and sand.

After Lagos, we steamed straight for Burutu on the Forcados River which forms part of the Niger Delta. This was Africa indeed, all the heat and the rain, mangroves and land crabs, creeks branching in every direction, islands of dense vegetation crowned with enormous forest trees aflame with crimson blossoms, huts on stilts, slim canoes shooting out into the river, shouting children plunging headlong into the yellow water, gambolling like small porpoises.

It was also a foretaste of those many scenes of utter confusion, of inextricable tangles, of chaos incarnate so typical of West Africa. There were five of us with roughly eighty loads each, making some 400 loads in all, not counting all the small personal impedimenta, which had to be moved from the Elder Dempster to the stern-wheeler in which the journey up to Mureji, at the confluence of the Niger and Kaduna Rivers, was to be made.

Who knows nowadays what a stern-wheeler even looks like? Take two sardine tins, lay them one on top of the other, run an old pipe stem through both, tie two empty reels of cotton on each side of the lower sardine tin and in the upper sardine tin put the largest cockroach you can find. Then launch the whole contraption on the swirling, racing waters of the third longest river in Africa. It was on to such a craft that we and all our belongings had to be transferred. In the process, each passenger had to check up on every one of his loads lest any should be left behind. As practically nothing could be bought in the country, the loss of a single load was a near disaster.

Though the stern-wheeler was for official transport only, the lower deck was already filled with Nigerian passengers, all dimly related to the crew or fulfilling some obscure nautical function. Women, children, babies, goats, fowls added to the babel. One wondered which was the most overwhelming, the heat or the noise. Then, suddenly, and equally typical of West Africa, chaos became order. A few more shouts and arguments broke the stillness and died away. The loads were neatly stacked in separate mounds on the stern-wheeler's upper deck, the deckchairs were put up, the boys brought teapots and the traditional tins of 'Rich Mixed' biscuits, the stern-wheeler shook herself, gave a warning hoot to the clustering canoes, the giant paddle-wheels turned in a welter of yellow foam and slowly we headed up the Niger River.

I try to remember what were my first impressions on this my first day in Africa. Fresh, unaccustomed eyes should have preserved a sharp-etched, brightly tinted picture, as of a newly discovered scene painted with vivid strokes in primary colours and observed with surprise and emotion. I can remember no impressions at all except one of complete familiarity. I was certainly neither blasé nor incurious nor indifferent, it was simply that all I saw had the imprint of the expected. And it must have been the same for many people: their fathers and grandfathers, elder brothers or uncles, had done the same kind of journeys, had seen canoes and parrots and spears, forests and deserts and marshlands. My father had been at the taking of Lagos in 1851 and, on the sloop *Pandora*, had captured the last Portuguese slaver; my uncles had been in India, a brother in China, another on the Pacific Station. I, like so many others who came out at that time, took it for granted that our lives would very likely be spent in foreign parts and all that we saw and heard was often but the echo of what was talked about in our own homes. Even as children, having no horror comics nor tales of spaceships and supermen, our reading was of stories of the sea, of explorers, of adventure in far-off lands.

For the few who were not already conditioned to strange countries, this journey was perhaps the best introduction a newcomer could have: whether you were conscious of it or not, the country soaked into you during those long days. You became familiar with the forest, the colours of leaf and blossom, the towering trunks and wide-spreading roots, the tangle of creeper and tree fern and intercoiled stems. You learnt the different sounds and smells of dawn and midday and night. You began even to guess at what might be the life in those poor huts clustering near the river bank, and you might notice how the shape of the huts changed or the style of the canoes or the features of the people as the stern-wheeler moved steadily on. After the forest had thinned out, you learnt the look of the low hills, pastures and scrub. The air dried and lightened and burnt. The people were different, you saw cattle, horses, markets on the river banks. You were bound to realize that Nigeria was not just a lump of Black Africa, but highly diversified geographically and equally differentiated ethnographically. This in itself was a valuable education that the swift-moving plane cannot impart.

As much as you learnt from watching the river bank glide slowly by, you learnt from listening to your fellow travellers. Naturally they talked 'shop', unendingly, argumentatively, enthusiastically, depressingly, acrimoniously. Only a soldier, seconded to the WAFF, and I had not been out before. Of the others, one was going to the far North, to the Holy North of Islam, walled cities, powerful Emirs; another was going to the Bauchi Plateau, the hilltop Pagans and the little beehive huts clinging to the rocks. My husband saw the country in terms of Transport: mileage, carriers, pack animals, roads to be built, equipment to be moved. The soldier and I listened while the paddles threshed and clanked, the shrill voices of the mammies on the lower deck rose and fell, the smell of palm-oil chop mingled with the half sweet, half sickly smell of water, leaves and mud. We sat bemused and perhaps a little awed by these men who had done and seen so much and made so little of it.

Looking back, I suppose a crowded stern-wheeler was discomfort incarnate. At anchor she was a furnace, although her upper deck had a sun-roof. Once started, what breeze there was only brought choking smells of mud and vegetation mingled with that of palm-oil as the mammies cooked precariously on the lower deck. The whole ship trembled continuously from stem to stern and seemed so racked between shuddering engines and thundering paddles that you expected her to fall apart every time the sudden bends of the river forced her round in a swift half-circle or a partly submerged tree trunk glanced against her fragile side. The Captain was usually a white man, often Swedish: according to legend they all were Counts. . . . Counts or not, they were wonderful with these ramshackle craft and haphazard crews. The actual steering was done by an African quarter-master clad in a loincloth and a Nigeria Marine cap. Though a wheel was foreign to him, the river was his own. Hour after hour, his gazed fixed unwaveringly ahead, he took us through the maze of waterways, islands, mangrove swamps and creeks that constitute the Niger Delta. The Count would occasionally appear, immaculate in white uniform, dignified, aloof.

There were two so-called cabins, that is to say square wooden boxes built up on the deck, empty of all furniture. Here you put up your bed and mosquito net, the enamel basin on the tripod stand, a camp-stool. Stacked in a corner was your personal luggage, for we were in the era of airtight tin cases, travelling baths with their wicker linings, red-lined helmets and green-lined umbrellas, spine-pads and tummy-bands, elaborate filters, water and Sparklet bottles, heavy leather-encased despatch boxes, every kind of wickerwork luncheon basket and – heaviest, ugliest and most invaluable of all – the black japanned Lord's lamp, complete with its kerosene tank and its Eiffel-Tower-like iron legs. On the decks were the tents and groundsheets, saddle boxes and cook boxes and, swamping everything else, the chop boxes.

Even chop boxes are now no more, yet in all those early days we could hardly have lived without them. Small, sturdy little three-ply – Venesta, it was called – cases, they held all the groceries and drinks needed for a twelve-month tour. Each one weighed 56 lbs., the regulation carrier's head-load. Each was named and numbered and padlocked and its contents listed on neat typed sheets. Several London and Liverpool firms had export departments. We always went to the Army and Navy Stores, and in all the years I dealt with them, not one mistake was ever made, though each order contained hundreds of items. In the *West African Cookery Book*, which my French sister-in-law, Geneviève Ruxton, and I later wrote together, we give a typical list of provisions for one man for one year. I have just glanced at it. Among the many necessities and semi-luxuries, I note with awe that a man would use in a year eighteen four-pound tins of loaf sugar, thirty-six seven-pound tins of flour, two half-pound tins of cloves, six half-pound bottles of curry powder, two small tins of Oakey's knife polish and three plum puddings. There were just a few stores like tinned milk or butter one could buy from the Niger Company, but their canteens were few and far between and the supply uncertain. It was simpler to be self-contained.

Apart from the 'cabins', there was a bathroom right aft between the paddle-wheels, filled with steam and spray and the roar of cascading waters. It was here the cockroaches, perchance an amphibious breed, had their stronghold, sallying forth in scurrying battalions as soon as night fell, giants of their kind.

We messed together on the deck, pooling the contents of our respective 'river boxes', which had been carefully packed with the essentials one would need for the first few days of the journey. The boys squabbled, the senior cook announced morosely: 'No fit make chop. Fire done die,' yet a meal appeared and the drinks were fairly cool, slung in the water-filled canvas buckets to catch the breeze. Of course, everyone grumbled – 'groused' was the word – but did anyone really mind very much? This was West Africa and if you did not like this sort of thing you had better go home again.

Shortly after dark a bell rang out. The engines slowed and stopped. The water cascading off the paddle-wheels quietened to a gentle stream, then to a murmur, then stopped. For a moment, what seemed utter stillness flooded over banks and river, from the starlit sky to our crowded decks. For that one moment, it held everything bound and motionless, without breath or thought. Then a frog croaked, a bird rustled in the branches, water swirled round a tree trunk, a child cried, cooking-pots rattled, someone strummed a little song on an African guitar, the anchor chain ran out with a clatter that echoed from one forest wall to the other, and all the noises of an African night burst in upon us.

Also the insects. Were they so very much worse than they are nowadays? Or were they like the sun-helmets which, one moment, were the ultimate protection against certain death and the next, the comic appendage of a few eccentrics? Insects are still numerous but even in the bush or near water, they are as nothing to the clouds that were encountered in those early days, to the soup-plate full of drowning ants, to the table-cloth dark with the wings of flying ants, to the constant boom as the big cockchafers hit wall or ceiling. Mosquitoes, tsetse fly, white ants, driver ants, were known and open enemies; it was the un-named multitudes whose warfare never ceased day or night that got one down. Though usually I could bear them philo-sophically enough, I think my only memories of well-nigh intolerable discomfort are related to insects in some form or other.

Early dawn saw the stern-wheeler on her way again. I remember calling at Onitsha to take on wood, our only form of fuel. Already Onitsha was its busy, bustling, vital self; already noise and movement was its climate. My husband and I walked up to the Roman Catholic Mission. After a glass of cool white wine drunk very quickly on a very hot morning, I have only a blurred vision of large bearded men in white cassocks who pressed baskets of fruit on us and whose handclasp filled one with courage and with confidence. The avenue of mangoes leading to the Mission was already planted. Today, the trees look immense as one moves out of the glare into their wide tunnel of shade.

Once more on our way up the river, there was a sudden stir among the white men. A high bluff rose out of the river on our right. Idah, the boundary between North and South! A sigh of relief went round. A few more revolutions of the hastening paddles, a long whistle, and we were in Northern Nigeria. Lokoja came next, then Mureji, where we left the stern-wheeler and two of our companions, transferred to steel canoes and poled up the Kaduna River to Barijoko, terminus of the strange little railway that jolted its way to Zungeru.

I have said I did not remember how long the journey took, but from my husband's letters during a previous tour, before we were married, I find he left Burutu on the 18th September, 1906, arrived at Lokoja on the 22nd, Mureji on the 23rd and Barijoko on the evening of the 24th – seven days in all. This was an exceptionally quick journey, made on the High Commissioner's yacht *Corona*. There was plenty of water both in the Niger and the Kaduna so that no transferring into poling canoes was necessary and, a further spur to speed, all Lokoja had come aboard on its way to the Zungeru Sports Week. ('There is a quite deafening din made up of squealing ponies, barking dogs, innumerable servants, *doki* boys and hangers on,' wrote my husband with irritation, comprehensible enough to those who remember the size of the *Corona*.)

But to return to this later journey. The Kaduna had got so silted up that the steel canoes had to stop a quarter of a mile from the 'railway station'. Carriers swarmed down on the loads and hurled them into the toy wagons of the Barijoko–Zungeru express, and two hours later Zungeru was reached.

Zungeru baked in the silence. Our bungalow was of the classic Public Works Department (PWD) pattern of which a few still survive: mounted on iron stilts some four feet above the ground, built of wood brought out from England, roofed with corrugated iron; three square rooms in a row and a verandah all the way round. The bungalow stood in its own grounds or rather, since the word 'grounds' suggests green lawns and shrubberies, it stood on its own laterite, a crescent-shaped drive in front, a few thin trees at the side, the kitchen and the boys' quarters behind. From the front verandah one looked, across a road leading to the barracks and the various headquarters offices, on to a monotony of stones and dry grass, quivering in the heat haze or skeleton dead beneath the moon.

The interior of the bungalow was both austere and fanciful. Since that day, I have lived in a number of similar dwellings and have never ceased to consider with wonder, almost with awe, the amount of misplaced ingenuity they represent. I have long wished to find a name for PWD architecture of the pioneer days. Perhaps Colonial Baroque (Early Period) would be the most apt. Though it boasted no columns or cupolas, no painted ceilings or gilded cherubs, each bungalow was a very riot of woodwork, a grand flowering of carpentry, of beams and rafters and shutters and transoms, of recesses and projections, of planks tongued and grooved laid at every conceivable angle and slant, of louvres and gratings and skirtings. The eyes rose to a forest of joists and cross-beams and sank amazed to the arsenic green and ox-blood red of the walls. Heavy brass hooks held back imaginary windows, vast bolts closed imaginary doors; verandah railings, in a symphony of dark and light green, crossed and criss-crossed in a pattern of endless variety.

Little could be done with the square, box-like rooms furnished with a few bits of curiously grey and tired-looking furniture. The broad front verandah, roofed over, with its green plants in native pots, its white Bida mats[7] and a few wicker chairs brought from the Canary Islands, was the pleasantest part of the house.

Pressure-lamps of various kinds gave a noisy and sadly unbecoming light until veiled by an ever-increasing swarm of insects; dim, humble, ever-faithful bush lamps burnt in kitchen and pantry. There was a *punkah* in the dining-room with a strange pleated skirt of khaki drill; a store-room into which were piled the year's provision of stores; a meat safe hung 'where breeze go catch him'. A neat row of native coolers, in which floated tins of butter and bottles of beer, took the place of the unused ice chest which was dense with cockroaches even fiercer than those which swarmed in the stern-wheeler's bathroom. Prisoners brought water in kerosene tins from half a mile away and attended to the sanitation, reduced to its simplest form of expression.[8]

The household staff was very much what it is today, only larger, more pervasive and often more devoted. Its efficiency was variable. On trek, the boys were wonders of endurance, good temper, ingenuity; in the bungalow, they were incalculable. Yet how could one expect them to deal with our meaningless, to them, manners and customs, all our paraphernalia of cups and saucers, sheets and pillow-cases? My husband had been fortunate in his steward Mommadu, almost too fortunate, for Mommadu would quietly transfer to a secret hoard anything of mine that he thought might be of use to his beloved master. Though the cook, 'Mr Brock', never attained the stature of my brother's 'Samson Okorike Esquire', he was a good cook and I keep an endearing memory of him one hot afternoon, sitting stark naked under the kitchen table, studying the coloured plates of lobsters and pheasants and fabulous desserts in his own vast green-bound volume of Mrs Beeton's Cookery Book. His salary of £3 a month and 2s. a week chop money was considered high. Mommadu had 30s. a month, the bevy of small boys and small-small boys got 5s. to 15s. a month.[9] The official rate for a carrier was 6d. a day when carrying a 56 lbs. load and 3d. a day when returning home empty. To justify these wages, it must be remembered that a man could live on 1d. a day and that a tenth of a penny could buy a meal for a child.

For the European, local food was cheap: 2s. 4d. for a good turkey, 5d. or so for a fowl. There was more game than now and excellent river fish. On the other hand, the imported groceries, a packed in special air-tight tins, the camp equipment, c ckery, linen, etc., were expensive items and the rough handling they got made their frequent renewal necessary. I

wonder how many of my sister-in-law's table-cloths, sliding off
a pack camel's back, still lie at the bottom of Lake Chad? Almost
everyone kept ponies, for polo or an occasional race meeting,
and practically all touring in the North was done on horseback. I
cannot remember the average cost of a decent pony,* but I know
the £30 my husband (always known as Arthur L.) offered for a
potential racehorse from Sokoto was considered a sensational
price.

Though cold store was unknown, meals were long and
copious and, alas, very often a holocaust of tins, though the
wiser host did his best to live off the country as much as possible
and nearly every station had its invaluable Mutton Club.[10] The
great lack was of fruit and vegetables: I remember nothing save a
few tomatoes and an occasional banana, pawpaw, and lime.

Social life was infinitely more formal than it is today. Cards
were left on me (how archaic that term sounds!); my husband
left cards on the Mess; invitations to a meal were contained in a
note and duly acknowledged; everyone dressed for dinner. The
cantonment (the Indian term was used, as also that of 'Cant.
Mag.') was scattered. If for some reason our dogcart was out of
action, bath-towels were flung over saddles and we rode to
dinner parties, I in a long low-necked dress, my husband in
white mess jacket and the French-grey cummerbund of
Northern Nigeria. Of course people dropped in informally for
drinks, and friends passing through camped in a corner of the
verandah; it was an unwritten law that travellers were housed
and fed and generally cared for, whoever they might be, but the
general social behaviour, as seen by me, the only married
woman in the station, had both the courtesy and the stiffness of
life in some old-fashioned English country-house.

I try to think what interests and relaxations there were in a
headquarters station like Zungeru in 1907. Possibly, left to
themselves, the civilians would have lacked the initiative to
tackle the physical obstacles involved even in the making of a
tennis court, but the military had more determination, more
labour at their disposal and, on the whole, more time. Tennis
was played; but polo was the chief attraction, whether the
ground was hard as stone or a sea of mud; leave could be

---

*The late Mr Kenneth Elphinstone informed me that in Yola, Muri and Bornu
Provinces, £3 was a high price for an average pony in the early days.

obtained for shooting or fishing; there was an occasional
gymkhana or race meeting. That was about the extent of the
station's resources. Intellectually, they were even fewer. There
was a daily Reuter. Newspapers arrived regularly, and after a
little time one no longer noticed that the news one read was a
month old. Was there not a Resident in a remote Province, re-
ceiving his *Times* in batches of twenty or thirty at a time, whose
steward, the perfect butler, carefully smoothed them out and,
one by one, laid them neatly on his master's breakfast table
every morning? The books we brought out were passed from
hand to hand. When a senior official came through, the talk was
often good, an earnest seeking to understand this country of
which we were but trustees. There was news of increments and
transfers, leaves and sailings. There was curiously little
reference to home affairs or doings, perhaps because the greater
number of the men were bachelors and, once away from Britain,
the link was not quite so strong as in the case of those who had
left wives and families behind.

Arthur L. played polo two or three times a week; on other
days, we drove the dogcart a few miles along the only road or
visited the Transport Lines. Sundays were reserved for letters
for the homeward mail, playing with the dogs and discussing the
ponies. Or, unconscious protest against our green and blood-red
walls and dull sticks of PWD furniture, we spent hours planning
how we would furnish the Leith-Ross ancestral home of Arnage
Castle, should some impossible miracle make Arthur L. its in-
heritor. I believe that, face to face with the stark realism of
Nigeria's early days, a streak of the fabulous running through
soberer thoughts was needed to keep one human. In every man's
mind, there was surely a castle in Spain to which he turned in
hours of aridity, or else he became a fanatic, either so enamoured
of the country or so hostile towards it that he lost all sense of proportion, all touch with his fellow men.

The only other women in Zungeru at that time were dear
Miss Mitchell who, with another Sister whose name I have forgotten, was in charge of the girls' Freed Slaves Home.[11] As
representing Freedom, it was a rather sad little place which
nevertheless gave me one of my most enduring and cherished
memories. In those Edwardian days, it was well-nigh unthink-
able that any well-brought-up young woman should not have a

maid, be she in South Kensington or in darkest Africa. Before my marriage, there had been a vast correspondence concerning this maid and by what means she was to be procured. Lady Lugard had been out for one tour, bringing her English maid with her. Apparently the maid had needed much more care than Lady Lugard herself, so that ruled out the possibility of having a European one. On the Coast, a few wives had trained African girls, but how get in touch with them? In the end, Miss Mitchell had descended on the Freed Slaves Home, carried off a young Fulani girl, and when I arrived, there was Howa to greet me. She must have been about fourteen, with all the Fulani pride of carriage, slim and straight, her gaze unwavering. She sat by the hour, her eyes fixed on the horizon above the stunted scrub, cool and still in the blazing heat. I cannot remember her ever doing any work except to fetch my thimble when I wanted to do some needlework. I see her still, delicately rummaging in my work-basket, then turning, the thimble poised upon her head, and gravely sinking on her knees before me. I never knew whether she liked me or not, but when, five years later, I met her again, married to a catechist,[12] clothed and dimmed and lifeless, we looked sadly at each other as friends much changed. In sudden fury, I gave her all the scents and coloured things I had, in protest against her new enslavement.

What did the men talk about? Very much as they have always talked, those who were keen on their job. The 'shop' was perhaps narrower, more provincial, more immediate. Economics scarcely came into it since there were few cash crops, no Marketing Boards or Development Grants, and not many foresaw any really important trade future for the North. There was of course the Bauchi tin, but the tin mines somehow remained curiously remote and self-contained, a world apart. Sir Percy Girouard[13] had come out in April 1907, as High Commissioner in succession to Sir Frederick Lugard who had left Nigeria in 1906, leaving Mr William Wallace[14] as Acting High Commissioner till Sir Percy's arrival. Sir Percy's project for the northern extension of the already existing Lagos–Ibadan railway was discussed with profound pessimism. What in all those miles of scrub and sand would be found for a railway to carry that could not be carried equally well and more cheaply on men's heads or in those bullock carts brought from India at Sir Frederick Lugard's command? It would be wiser to build more roads, metalled and drained and bridged so that such wheeled transport could be used even throughout the wet season. Speed was not yet a dictator of men's plans and outlook. The country was far from inert, but its vastness had the power to impose its own tempo on the handful of white men.

Present-day parties and politics did not exist. On the other hand, 'Policy' loomed large. The theory of Indirect Rule was accepted by most and, as seen from headquarters, it seemed the only feasible one. For the man on the spot it cannot have been so simple, trying to find his way along the devious paths of intrigue and jealousies, learning to know when to stand back and when to interfere, attempting to assess what was good in the existing regime, feudal and autocratic as it was, and what was inexcusably bad and unjust. He had also to learn the language and, if stationed in a Muslim Emirate, know something of *The Koran* and of Muslim law. It seems now to be the fashion to condemn the whole idea of Indirect Rule and to blame Lord Lugard for all the difficulties which arose later in the North. It is possible the policy was too sweeping, that the large Pagan minorities should have been more considered, that there should have already been long-term planning for future development, trade, education. But do these critics even begin to realize what were the conditions then? I think I am right in saying that, apart from the Army, there were some forty Political Officers (Residents, Assistant Residents) to run a roadless, partly mapless country of ten or more million inhabitants of different races, religions, languages and customs. The death and invaliding rate was so high that officials had to be constantly moved to fill sudden vacancies; money was always short; at home, public interest was non-existent.

It might be said that a young wife, sitting on a verandah in Zungeru, could not know much about what was going on, but I was a good listener, nearly every official passed through Zungeru, and every conversation ended in 'shop'. I look back after all these years, seeing more clearly our mistakes, prejudices, weaknesses, and yet claim 'there were giants in those days'.

Naturally it was about my husband's Department that I knew most as to actual details. His letters from Zungeru before we were married had given me an almost day-to-day account of its beginnings and I marvelled that anything so coherent and efficient had arisen out of that first chaos. When Sir Frederick Lugard appointed him Chief Transport Officer in 1904, the only road in the country was the still unfinished section between Zungeru and Zaria. It was proposed to use it for bullock cart transport if this proved feasible, but its many unbridged rivers and streams made it a dry season road only.

This road was nearly finished in December 1904. In the meantime, the Department administered a picturesque assortment of carriers and camels, pack-donkeys, mules, ponies and oxen.[15] Track had to be kept of their attendants, feeding-stuffs, distance covered, nature of loads, and the exact Department to which the loads belonged so that it could be debited with the transport costs. One can imagine the acrid correspondence with the Posts and Telegraphs Department over a telegraph pole lost on the way to Bornu, or with the Public Works Department regarding a bag of cement dropped into the Gongola River. Military patrols had also to be supplied at a moment's notice; French and German Boundary Commissions loomed suddenly out of space; even a Missionary Bishop's ponies had to be shod.

As it was impossible to put Transport Officers in every centre, the Residents of Provinces were for the time being obliged to look after that portion of the transport allotted to or passing through their Provinces. Little money was given the Department and only the strictest accountancy could keep it within its Vote. One could not blame Arthur L., upon whom rested the whole responsibility, yet it was impossible not to sympathize with the pathetic plea of a tired Resident asking whether it really mattered if it were Audu or Ahmadu who drew 2s. chop money, or with my brother's humble telegram: 'Beg Muri Province be exempted from Animal Transport.' The reply was a stern negative, until a little later the presence of tsetse fly decided the question in my brother's favour.

All sorts of odd items appear in Arthur L.'s letters: 'The Cape Cart, the one Government bought from Lord Scarbrough, has arrived, a very fine vehicle, too good for Government purposes – will use it myself, do not know what else to do with it.' 'The

Secretary of State asks for a map showing the tsetse belts.'
'Captain Condon just down from Katsina, five days' march
from Kano, with a string of camels and five hundred oxen.' 'Am
to see High Commissioner with reference to the carriage of
officers' kit within cantonments. A question which I believe has
been under discussion for some six years.' And I believe,
seventy years later, still is!

Considering the distances, the incidents of the road, bush
fires, floods, bolting camels, fallen ponies, sick carriers, the little
supervision that was possible, and often the value and the
fragility of the goods transported, it was remarkable how little
was lost or damaged.

In accordance with Sir Frederick Lugard's wishes, pack
saddles, harness and two-wheeled bullock carts had been imported from India. A small contingent of Transport and
Veterinary Officers, as well as Indian clerks, Naiks and artificers
had been brought over at the same time. The experiment was
never a success; in a few years it had been dropped and the
Indians drifted home, though there had been some good men
among the artificers and Naiks, and the Transport Lines just
across the Kaduna was the showpiece of Zungeru when I was
there.

As High Commissioner, Sir Percy Girouard lost no time in getting to know the country. Letters from Arthur L. give a breathless account of His Excellency's first tour, begun nine days after
his arrival in Zungeru. The first three days were occupied giving
dinner parties to all the Europeans: 'shockingly bad ones'
grumbles Arthur L., 'his ADC, quite a youth, will have to buck
up.' Luckless ADCs of those days, thrown into a bare
Government House, no more than a larger, gaunter bungalow,
without a single amenity beyond the *punkah* in the dining-room
(Sir Frederick Lugard had hardly noticed whether or not he had
a chair to sit on), with an untrained staff and a vast but diminish-
ing store of crockery and cutlery. It diminished because it was
customary for a guest to bring with him his own steward, whose
loyalty to his master was shown by the number of forks or
spoons he could purloin during the course of a meal and which
next morning, much like a faithful dog laying a dead rat at his

master's feet, he would proudly bring to the breakfast table. 'Lion, behold what I bring you!' I seem to remember a series of ADCs throughout the years, all very young, very much alike, fair-haired, blue-eyed, charmingly mannered but with a worried frown that never left their candid brows.

Nine days later, Sir Percy went on tour to Zaria and Kano, taking Arthur L. with him. For the instruction of those members of the present generation who are horrified by Nigerian roads, shocked by the absence of air-conditioning in Catering Rest-Houses and the lack of a cold store in every hamlet, I cannot resist quoting some of Arthur L.'s letters describing conditions which a High Commissioner took in his stride.

> *27th April, 1907. Kagara.* We left Zungeru yesterday and we trek to Ringa Depot [a Transport Department depot on the cart road to Zaria] at 4 a.m. tomorrow, doing $27\frac{1}{2}$ miles. Our party is composed of H.E., Murray his A.D.C., Dr Cameron Blair, Fletcher, the O.C. Escort and myself. As we are travelling fast and must be back in Zungeru on the 23rd May, we are using carriers, 150 of them.
>
> *Koriga River, 2.30 p.m.* Since yesterday have been messing with H.E. – the more I see of him, the more I like him. It was late last night before I finished my work and we were on trek at 3.30 a.m. today, reaching this place, 22 miles, at 10.30 a.m. Charles Orr, Resident Zaria, has just come in.[16]
>
> *3rd May.* For the first time since leaving Zungeru we will have some sleep, for reveille will not be until 4.30 a.m. A guard of honour is coming some 6 miles out of Zaria, also the Emir with a large following. We will meet them about 6 o'clock. We will leave all open loads at Zaria and go on as light as possible. The wretched servants and the following in general are not having too happy a time but it cannot be helped and there has been no complaint on their part.

Kano was reached on 8 May and the return journey was begun the following day by a more westerly road passing through Yelwa, Kariari (Karaye?) and Rogo to Zaria.

> From Zaria we take a road to the east of the cart road and will proceed through that part of the country where the pro-

jected railway will run. The trek has been uneventful except for two marches at two and three a.m. At Bebeji, two marches from Kano, we were met by Major Festing, Acting Resident, Kano Province.[17] Yesterday evening we were treated to a sudden tornado without rain. It came up without warning and with disastrous results and as we were on loose and dusty ground we had a dirty time of it. H.E.'s tent was blown down on top of him just as he was going to take a bath. My tent, with the help of the servants, stood up. I was in my bath at the time and was compelled to remain there assisting in holding up the tent pole – I was a shocking sight, black as the blackest native. H.E. took it in good part and as nothing could be done with his tent, he helped to ram down the pegs of mine. This morning, it rained throughout our trek but now that we are suitably clad, it was most welcome and laid the dust. 5 p.m. It is nearly dark. I must go and see to the horses – we have eighteen with us.

16th May, 5 p.m. We are camped outside a small Gwari Pagan village with an unpronounceable name – it is raining in torrents. We arrived at Zaria on the 13th and left the following day. This morning we were forced on account of lack of supplies slightly to alter our route. Our column has been increased, Captain Orr joining us at Zaria, and Kempthorne (the Intelligence officer) yesterday, so we total something like 250 people. Nothing of interest, the country is much wooded, the roads mere bush paths, food difficult. Since leaving Zaria, we have marched respectively 21, 19 and 18½ miles and tomorrow we have to do 28, there being no nearer place where we can obtain supplies. After tomorrow, we will be in better country and should reach Zungeru on the 23rd, the date fixed on.

If naught else, to be High Commissioner of Northern Nigeria was an endurance test.

I have said that social life was formal: I have just found two unidentifiable photographs of a group at what was presumably a race meeting, either at Lokoja or at Zungeru. The men wear helmets and are coated and trousered, collared and tied, or in the most correct of riding kit. The four women present sit in a group apart, in summery but long-skirted, high-necked, long-sleeved dresses, elaborate hats tilted at a becoming angle. The empty seat of honour is a wicker settee from Las Palmas. Rough canvas shelters, horse-boys, a few soldiers, a long low line of hills form the background. A third photograph is easily recognizable as that of the Governor of German Togoland, Graf von Zech, watching polo at Zungeru. Affable and smiling, he sits next to Sir Percy Girouard who, in a Homburg hat and white trousers, looks as if he had just walked out of the casino at Deauville. I sit on the German Governor's left, very prim in a dark coat and skirt, holding Square Face, a lively puppy we had just acquired. Next to me, also prim and very neat, is Miss Mitchell, in dark-skirted riding habit, white jacket and helmet. Behind the mild and lovable Secretary to the Administration, Marcus Beresford,[18] stands ramrod straight, fierce in uniform and cropped hair, the German Governor's ADC, Erich von Reitzenstein. Arthur L. in his riding clothes has come straight from some smart point-to-point and those grouped around him are not far behind in correctness of attire.

Ridiculous as it may seem to find moral significance in a casual group photograph, one begins to understand how it was that such a handful of men could dominate the land. Collars and ties were a foolish social convention, yet, in the context of that merciless heat, the obedience to the convention took on an heroic aspect. Backbone was required to fasten a collar stud; backbone was what the country required. Today, perhaps less courage, tenacity, fortitude, are required so the conventions can be neglected. In those days, in so great a loneliness, yet watched so closely by alien eyes, too much lowering of standards would have been dangerous. Rudyard Kipling is now decried but often what he wrote was wise:

'By all you will or whisper, by all you leave or do,
The silent, sullen peoples will judge your God and you.'

Not only was each white man's character at stake, to be made or marred by his Nigerian experience, but the actual lives of his compatriots depended to a great extent on his behaviour. We were lucky in finding the African, on the whole, neither silent nor sullen but, very naturally, Emirs and Chiefs resented our coming. Even among the lesser people, a stupid act or careless phrase could easily inflame a suspicious crowd. Much already had been done between 1900 and 1907 to establish our influence and, though force had been necessary on a number of occasions, in the long run it was the will-power of the white man which held the country together and kept the greatest evil, the slave raids, in check. So far from home and with such slow communications, many decisions had to be taken on the spot, and if things went wrong, it was the man on the spot who was to blame. As far as the Army officers in charge of native troops were concerned, they were wonderfully lighthearted, considering how often death moved among them, sometimes in grim shape. Gathering up their men, rifles, ammunition and possibly a machine-gun, they went off on a 'scrap' with the same enthusiasm they would have shown had it been a meet of hounds on a winter's morning, and with no more anger against the black man they were about to punish than they had felt towards the English fox. But if a fox had robbed a hen roost and some local Chief had raided a village for slaves, well, he was fair game and that was all there was in it. Rough justice? Perhaps, but it was a justice the African understood, and more real and just than the present-day twists and turns of clever lawyers or the blind application of a Western legal system by too-punctilious judges.

Zungeru was so much an artificial town that there was little direct contact with the African except as soldier, policeman, Government labourer, or house-boy. The clerks were either from Sierra Leone or from Southern Nigeria and formed a little world of their own. The few peasants seen were Gwari Pagans, farming the ungrateful soil with primitive instruments.

There was not much a white woman could do within the narrow bounds of cantonment life. Nevertheless, I think with shame and regret of how little I took advantage of that year in Zungeru. But I was haunted by apprehension of some near disaster and could not shake off its crippling effect.

The few times we were able to go on short tours were a delight. We rode down to Minna – no shrieking railway engines then and clanking wagons, merely a straggle of huts in a wide cup of the hills. It was Easter Sunday – the rains were approaching and there was a single cloud high up in the sky. Straight from the empty glare of Zungeru, I thought I had never seen anything so beautiful. We climbed at dusk to a cluster of huts among the rocks. Not a soul was to be seen. From high ground beyond the hamlet, there was a Mountains-of-the-Moon landscape of small stony hills and rocks and boulders, ghost-like beneath heavy clouds and quick-falling darkness. Nearby, a startled hunter gripped his dog and quickly drew back into the deeper shadow of a rock. Arthur L. called out a greeting, but man and dog only crouched closer to the rock and stared in wild-eyed fear. Bow and arrows, naked body, snarling dog, the barren darkening landscape, it was all the Africa of the story-books, a picture I have never forgotten.

Another comes to mind, from somewhere beyond Tegina: out of a haze of gold dust, a herd of grey-white, wide-horned Fulani cattle came down to drink. Leading them was a huge black bull, and astride the bull was a very small boy, head thrown back, shouting with glee, beating the large flanks with a slender reed. A little further on, we came to the encampment. The men were away with the cattle; the women slipped behind the huts, afraid. Then they came nearer, touched us gently, suddenly realized I was a woman and burst into lovely rippling laughter. All their movements were discreet and graceful; their speech lilting and melodious. As we rode away, a Fulani woman found a few words of Hausa:[19] 'Come again! Come again!'

A new road had been surveyed from Bauchi to Loko on the Benue, chiefly for the benefit of the tin mines. Arthur L. wished to inspect it and we had planned to do a really long tour of the Bauchi Plateau as soon as the rains had lessened, but in August 1908 Arthur L. died of blackwater fever and I returned to England. Of our party of five who had sailed from Liverpool thirteen months before, I was the only one left.

PART II: 1910–1913

Little had changed in Northern Nigeria between Sylvia Leith-Ross's departure in 1908 and her return in 1910. Sir Percy Girouard, railway engineer as well as colonial administrator, had been succeeded as Governor by Sir Hesketh Bell. Girouard's pet project, the Baro–Kano railway, had nearly reached its destination and was being joined up with the Southern Nigerian railway. Meanwhile, though now linked by both river and rail, the two Nigerias continued to be separately administered.

★

> The English were quite right. One had to dress for dinner. One needed a symbol, some external sign, to assist daily remembrance of what one was.
>
> Elenore Smith Bowen
> *Return to Laughter*

My first visit to Nigeria had ended in a personal disaster, yet through that disaster was created the bond which has held me to the country for sixty years. Whatever other activities I may have had, sooner or later some outer or inner necessity would send me back, often gladly, sometimes reluctantly, but always with the knowledge I could not do otherwise than go. It was so on this first occasion. My own private world had come to an end. Nigeria remained. Having no more cause for fear, I found that I loved her. But how go back? There was no room then for the private visitor or the casual traveller. I could go out under the Colonial Nursing Service but the training would be long. I had no experience of teaching. My brother was Resident of Muri Province, astride the Benue. His headquarters had recently been moved from desolate Amar on the north bank to the rather pleasanter Ibi on the south bank. He and his wife would willingly have me, but even if permission were obtained to travel alone, there must be some good reason for what was then an adventurous undertaking, and one which might also mean unnecessary responsibility or anxiety for overworked officials.

Through the haze of indecision came a sudden lilt of women's voices and a ripple of laughter. Instantaneously, compellingly, I remembered the Fulani encampment beyond Tegina and the woman who had cried: 'Come again!' I had always liked languages. The little work that had been done on Fulani was mainly in French and German. Here was, not a mere excuse, but a valid aim.

Sir Frederick Lugard was in London and it was his permission I had to obtain.[1] I hardly hoped he would agree. Even to me, the idea sounded preposterous. There was no accommodation anywhere; what transport there was, was needed for

Government officials; the country was unsettled; the climate still dangerous. As to Sir Frederick himself, I had only met him once at his home at Abinger and had always thought of him as somewhat inhuman, indifferent to any personal consideration, and that he would certainly be adverse to the idea of a young woman straying alone through the Muslim North. Having listened to my few words, I do not know what moved him to answer, instantly, and with that rare smile of his: 'Go, my child.'

That was in 1910. I went first to Zungeru, then down again to Lokoja and, since the water in the Benue was high, by stern-wheeler to Ibi.

Why did the journey seem so much simpler than those I have undertaken much more recently? Even for someone like myself, sure of the assistance of any white man I met (albeit that there were very few of them), there were always moments when you found yourself alone, with only yourself to count on, in one of those bedrock situations so common to Nigeria, which only your own patience or obstinacy or ingenuity or tact or humour – especially humour – could clear up. By the time you had reached your journey's end, you had a sense of achievement and, difficulties and discomforts forgotten, a self-congratulatory surge of elation. It is true that in these days you still have a sense of victory over fearful odds when you succeed, say, in retrieving your 'Unaccompanied Baggage' from Kano Airport Customs, but there is no elation in it, merely irritation that so much energy has to be expended, in spite of so many, and such expensive, facilities.

It is also true that on this first occasion of my return to Nigeria, much of the embankment of the light railway between Barijoko and Zungeru had been washed away by the rains, so that only a hand trolley could keep to the rails lightly looped over the gaps. Every now and then we had to get off and the two white men and myself stepped gingerly from sleeper to sleeper, trying not to see the drop beneath. Yet even this uneven progress seemed less irksome than bouncing from corrugation to corrugation along, shall we say, the main Makurdi–Wamba road fifty years later.

Zungeru itself was unchanged. Already in 1908, Sir Percy

Girouard, the Governor of Northern Nigeria, had laid down that no more building should be done there, though I do not think that the Kaduna site had yet been decided on as the next, and this time, permanent, headquarters for Northern Nigeria. The Baro–Kano extension was making rapid progress. 'The blessed old B.K. Railway is coming along like wild-fire,' wrote a soldier, 'but the blackguards have gone and cut a hole right across our parade-ground, together with some half-dozen drains. Some little ingenuity is necessary in drill now, otherwise one discovers one's whole parade disappearing down a drain or falling over an embankment.' The Army carried weight in those days. Could it be expected to move its parade-ground for a mere railway?

I stayed a few days with Marcus Beresford, still Secretary to the Administration. I met old friends of Arthur L. and found with deep gratitude that they looked on me as if I still 'belonged'. I rode up early one morning to Lion Kopje looking over the polo ground. Next time I went that way, years later, a quick rush of antelope parted the high grass on the polo ground and there were leopard tracks between the rusted iron sockets that had held the gates of Government House.

The journey back to Lokoja was uneventful. How magnificent was the view from Pati Hill, overlooking the confluence of the Niger and the Benue. Both were in flood, seemingly immense, pouring out of unknown horizons. Of Lokoja itself, still presumably an important station, I can remember nothing, save a sleepless night and a true story that was stranger than fiction. A railway foreman, who had worked under Sir Percy Girouard in South Africa, decided he would like to do so again in Nigeria. Alone, unarmed, totally ignorant of what route to follow, with little money, no equipment, no knowledge of native languages, he started to walk. He had a compass; he headed north, then west. He found Sir Percy at Lokoja, reported, and asked for work, as unconcernedly as if he were still in Cape Town. When he had been signed on, Sir Percy asked him how he would like to celebrate his safe arrival after so many hardships. 'Give me all the drink I want for twenty-four hours,' was the reply. That night, I was to sleep on board the stern-wheeler which would take me up the Benue. The South African foreman had been accommodated in a launch alongside, there being no available quarters on shore. Already, judging from the joyous shouts and songs, his request had been fully and blissfully granted.

For two days, a detachment of the Northern Nigeria Regiment and two officers travelled with me, on their way to some unremembered 'scrap'. Rifles, ammunition, gear of all kinds, encumbered the tiny deck. I had the only 'cabin', the usual square, empty box. The officers put up their beds and tin baths in any corner their boys could find. They seemed at home with their men and with the country. Once more, one was reminded of some country squire's sons setting off, with a gamekeeper or two and a squad of local beaters, to shoot over the stubble fields they had known from childhood.

Soon after they landed, I went down with a bad go of fever. Against the hurtling current, the black Captain, sleepless, drove the rickety boat day and night, hoping to find a doctor at the small Government station at Abinsi. Every now and then, I would dimly recognize him at the foot of my camp-bed. 'Ma no dead yet?' he would softly enquire. When found, the Abinsi doctor was anxious kindness itself. I can hear him still, as, sitting on a camp-stool with a tin of Ideal milk, a bottle of brandy and a basket of eggs on the floor beside him, he prepared an egg flip as best he could, muttering: 'Shocking business! – shocking business!' and an occasional 'Damn!' as egg after egg broke into that indescribable mess which only Nigerian eggs can achieve. He wanted to bring me ashore, but the worst was over and I had been taught not to be a nuisance.

On we went. From my camp-bed, I could hear strange throbbings and clankings. Once again, the Captain appeared. 'Engine plenty sick. Live for die.' As he spoke, there was a crash and a hiss of escaping steam. Then silence. 'He die,' said the Captain, sadly.

The stern-wheeler swung helplessly in the flooded river till she was somehow edged into the quieter water near the bank. It was only half a day's run to Ibi. Several canoes were lashed to our sides. One was got ready with as much comfort as the crew could devise, a grass mat as shelter, a tarpaulin laid along the bottom. Almost too weak to move, I crept along the deck. Three mail-bags lay there. My one wish was to reach the canoe and lie down again. Almost roughly, the Captain stopped me. 'Mails go first!' The meek, kindly little man spoke with a strange authority, suddenly invested with the dignity of transmitter of the orders of the King of England. He was right. Wherever you were, whatever the conditions, His Majesty's mails took precedence. I stood back at once, rebuked, and curiously impressed.

In those days and for many years, the simpler minds had a hazy but very real conviction that the King of England sat upon a throne, a crown upon his head, and knew all that happened in Nigeria, to black and white alike. I think the white men themselves, even in their tiny numbers in those huge solitudes, had a sense of being the direct representatives of the power of Britain. It worked both ways: it made often for high-handed action; it made also for high moral courage.

Ibi, the new headquarters of the very extensive area then known as Muri Province, was a featureless straggle on the left bank of the Benue. To the south, the country was flat, covered with coarse grass and scrub. To the north, across the wide river, strange square hills rose singly, straight out of the plain. The sunsets were vast and incandescent; the nights full of the croaking of frogs, the chirp of crickets, and sometimes a lion's roar.

As Resident, my brother had a five-roomed bungalow, a unique and much prized brick wall originally built for a Niger Company Agent, and a flagstaff.[2] Looking back, I remember it as a cheerful place, with people always coming and going – a man just in from the bush – another going up the Benue to Yola – a Roman Catholic Father from the newly opened Mission at Shendam. Geneviève, my French sister-in-law, was a friend to all. She was amused and interested by everything. Her French wit expressed itself in charming, only occasionally halting, English; her taste could make something out of nothing, and banquets out of mudfish and the humble fowl. She accompanied my brother on all his frequent tours, courageous and tireless, and even her sun-helmet took on an air of the rue de la Paix.

My brother was good at his job of taming these remote and half-known pagan tribes of the Benue valley. He had a sure intuition of what was going on in those black heads, behind those bright, unblinking eyes which told you nothing. He was very firm with the more enlightened Muslim chiefs, very patient with the frightened bush people. The difficult Munshi (I do not know at what precise moment a Munshi became a Tiv!)[3] were in his Province but only a few times did he have trouble with them. He was fortunate also in the Assistant Residents – the old name for District or Assistant District Officers – under him. Devoted and keen, they carried out much the same duties as did their successors, only with greater difficulty since much of the Province was hardly known. The distances were great; touring on horseback, on foot, or by canoe, was slow and wearisome.

Yet perhaps the best memories of Nigeria any of us have are of those days spent on tour. In spite of fatigue, monotony, discomfort, they were strangely happy. You have but to read Captain Hastings' *Nigerian Days** to recapture for a moment the spell of those long hours.[4] And above all, they were precious in that, whether you wished it or not, the country entered into you. The dust, heat, torrential rain, sickly smell of swamp or rushing *harmattan*,† penetrated and possessed you. You could not escape them – nor could you escape learning something of the very heart of this alien land.

Today, travelling by plane or car, who has time to appraise the crops, to know what was being sold in the market, to hear what was being said in the villages? What is surprising is how much the District Officers did know, and how much they still cared for the man in the bush.

All the same, in spite of happy moments, the life was a stern one. There were sudden hostilities, quick and sometimes unduly harsh reprisals; personal quarrels and jealousies among the Europeans; sudden illness, and the almost uncontrollable irritabilities induced by climate and discomfort. Some men were unfitted for the life, the type of work, and especially for the loneliness of the bush stations. And indeed, the demand on endurance, good humour, strength of will, moral integrity, was great. Not only were these virtues necessary, they were fruitless without enthusiasm. The job the Political Officer was called upon to

---

*Or, more recent, Sir Bryan Sharwood Smith's admirable *But Always as Friends*.

†The *harmattan* is the cold, sand-laden wind that blows down from the North from December to February, and can be felt as far away as the coast.

do was not a static one, a mere question of keeping law and order, stopping slave-trading, inter-tribal wars, preventing extortion. He had to be a jack of all trades, administering justice and experimenting with coffee plantations; mapping his district and introducing vaccination; laying out a market, clearing the bush to make some sort of road; watching that the newly-laid telegraph wire was not cut down by the tribesmen to make bangles for their wives. There was no one to turn to for help or advice; no form of communication swifter than a runner; no acceptable excuse if he failed to do his best. Often the people he administered would listen attentively while he explained his plans. They would seem to understand and agree, but when the time came to carry them out, there was no co-operation, only an obstinate sitting-back. 'Our fathers' fathers farmed – or built – or cut down trees – in this way. It was good for them. It is good for us.'

Not only was infinite patience needed but also an inborn comprehension of the countryman's mind. And this – immense asset – was what many of these early Political Officers had. Possibly the largest number of them were sons of country squires, country clergy, or Service people retired to the country.[5] They had been brought up in the country, taught to shoot by the old gamekeeper, to ride by the family coachman. They had climbed for birds' nests with the village boys, gone ferreting with the farmers' sons. Consciously or unconsciously, they had absorbed some knowledge of fields and woods and crops. They knew the slow talk of the countryside, and understood its resistance to change, its prejudices against new methods.

They had also learnt the rights and responsibilities of those set in authority and they knew how to command, easily, certain they would be obeyed. They administered justice as they had seen their fathers do among the poachers and petty thieves of their own countryside, without searching or questioning, but with an innate sense of what was just and what was unjust.

A haphazard training for men destined to rule millions? At that stage, could a better one have been found?

My own life at Ibi was chiefly occupied by Fulani studies. Of course, it was not an ideal area, but I was fortunate in finding two intelligent *malams*,[6] one who had come from Sokoto, the other from Yola. Audu, the Resident's interpreter, was the go-between, and I can never be sufficiently grateful for the patience and enthusiasm of those three men who led me through the maze of a rich and lovely language. I was only an amateur at the task, but I was an honest one, and since so little had been done, even my small contribution seemed worth while.

At the end of the year, my brother and Geneviève went on leave and I left with them, going later to Paris to study under Professor Maurice Delafosse at the Ecole des Langues Orientales.[7]

★ ★ ★

I returned to Ibi early in 1913. How clearly incidents of my visit still stand out when more important sequences have been forgotten.

A fellow passenger on his first tour was going to Muri Province as Assistant Resident, together with a large, vivacious, and charming bull terrier. We travelled up the Benue together, and as the water was very low, we each had a steel canoe and a dug-out for our own loads. These canoes, sometimes glorified with the name of house-boats, were simple affairs of two compartments divided by a partition, one for a camp-bed, the other for a chair and camp-table. At one end, there was sometimes even a tiny kitchen from which one's cook produced corned beef, fried fish, or even a miracle of curried fowl. There was a light sunroof and canvas curtains on both sides which could be let down to keep out the glare. The polers (using paddles in deeper water) clustered in the bows. The hell-man (a mingling of headman and helmsman) stood in the stern, his long steering paddle trailing behind him. In spite of his skill, we stuck again and again in the shallow water between the vast banks of burning sand. The days were long; discomfort great.

For better or for worse, people got to know each other pretty well after a week or two of Nigerian travel.

In Armar Auchinleck, no one could have had a pleasanter, more eager companion, with a deep gravity behind his light-heartedness which surprised in one so young. Already, on the

Elder Dempster coming out, I had noticed how he, the most un-assuming of newcomers, had made an unexpected impression. His contemporaries seemed to want his good opinion; senior men troubled to seek him out and to pass on to him whatever of their experience could be useful to him. People said of him: 'There's something about him . . .' and stopped short, wondering.

On the journey up the river, we talked endlessly about Nigeria, the future of the country, our own duties and responsibilities. Law and order had to be established. That the British should be the ones to do so, we – being of our generation – did not doubt for an instant, but it had to be done with equity and understanding. The Empire had to be upheld, but it must stand for justice and freedom. That Nigeria should grow up, and grow out of the Empire, was a possibility still too remote to be envisaged by us.

In the meantime, we had a problem of our own. We had always dressed for dinner. This was a rule that could not be broken, either at home or abroad, at sea or on shore, in the Arctic Circle or on the Equator. But alas, there was very little space indeed in our steel canoes. A compromise was necessary. Every night, we tied up at the edge of a sandbank and dined – we would not have used a less formal word – by the light of a Lord's lamp, high on its tripod. One evening Armar would change his bush shirt and I would change my khaki skirt; the next, I would change my white blouse and Armar would change his khaki breeches. Between the two of us, we had obeyed our code and had upheld our own and our country's dignity.

I laugh now (as would, quite naturally, all the younger generation) at the seriousness with which we took these symbols. Then I realize how sensible it was (I am glad to know an American writer, unfettered by tradition, who agrees with me). When you are alone, among thousands of unknown, unpredictable people, dazed by unaccustomed sights and sounds, bemused by strange ways of life and thought, you need to remember who you are, where you come from, what your standards are. A material discipline represents – and aids – a moral discipline.

Past Abinsi (Makurdi was but a small village, quite unknown), Armar's canoe turned down into the Katsina River which would lead him to his station of Katsina Ala (spelt Katsena Allah on the map of 1906), as lonely a spot as one could find. A little later, when I had reached Ibi, there was a happy letter from him. He liked the people; he had plenty to do; the bull terrier was well; he could see the river from his house. 'I am like a king.' He was only in Nigeria for one tour. Early in the 1914 war, his mother wrote: 'Armar was shot through the heart, at midday, on a bright Sunday, leading his men.' It would have been inconceivable that he should have died in a less shining way.

I went on alone, ever more slowly, though the polers worked well. Hour after hour their poles splashed in the water, rose glistening, silver dripping, and splashed again. They sang shrilly, high above the burning stillness, and the canoe swayed slightly as their bodies bent to each downward stroke. We saw no one, save an occasional trading canoe or a fisherman and, at sunset, great crowds of birds coming down to drink. From a distance, they resembled some fantastic multitude in fancy dress, dancing on a pale gold sand in a pale pink light.

Late one evening, we tied up as usual at the rim of a sandbank, having passed a solitary light we took to be that of a fisherman's camp. It was pitch dark save where the Lord's lamp made a pool of light. Even more than usual, I had the sense of being outside the recognizable world, apart from all known experience. I had just finished my meal when a slight sound made me look up. Poked through the wall of night was a black hand, and in the black hand was a white visiting card. I doubt whether anything could have appeared more astounding at that moment than that correct, commonplace, pasteboard card. On it was engraved in German the name of the *kaiserlicher* and *königlicher* Chief State Adviser on Tropical Forestry and, added in pencil, the request to be permitted to call on the *gnädige Frau*.[8] A moment later, a neat, white-clad, middle-aged German stood in front of me. Too astonished to speak, we circled round the Lord's lamp, bowing to each other again and again, until curiosity overcame us and we sat down to explain our presence. He spoke some English, I remembered some German. He was a nice man, with immense knowledge and no understanding. He was amazed that I could travel alone, without escort, for though he spoke highly of the potential resources of the country and appreciated the goodwill of the officials he had met, he was positively contemptuous of our methods of dealing with the African. 'How do you think it possible that you should get your polers to work when I cannot?' He became plaintive. 'They will not start in the morning and they stop before the sun has set!' I could not help thinking of my own crew pushing through the dawn, of their song in the midday blaze, of the ripples of starlit steel as they urged the canoe through the darkness. He went on: 'You do not know how to govern, you English. You are not severe enough – *nicht streng genug*,' and he pounded with his fist upon the table. 'I tell you,' he repeated, glaring,*'sie sind nicht streng genug*! Look at those polers. I beat them and I beat them, and yet they will not work for me!'

Early next morning, the German's canoes were still nosing sleepily into the bank. With a chuckle of amusement, my men pushed off, lifted high their poles, thrust deep, and shot out into the stream, pearl-grey beneath the dawn.

We had no more encounters except with crocodile and hippo and always, at sunset, on the huge sandbanks that strange multitude of birds. I knew no name for most of them, but there seemed to be every variety of crane, heron, egret, flamingo, secretary-bird, crown-bird, pigeon, wagtail, birds of every size and colouring, exquisitely beautiful or fantastically grotesque. They made no sound save for the soft rustling of their wings as they opened and closed them in some intricate and delicate game. No, not a game, rather was it a marvellous ballet, for the birds moved as if commanded by a single instinct. They bowed and circled, spread wide wings as if for a flight suddenly arrested, sprang a few feet into the air, advanced and retreated, seemingly never losing their places in the ordered sequence. The passage of my two canoes never for an instant disturbed them, so sunk were they in some ancient and happy dream of a world of wings and rustling feathers. As the sun sank, all their colours turned to pink and the sandbanks dimmed to palest gold. It was an enchantment never to be forgotten.

A couple more days and Ibi was reached. Ibi had not changed. Perhaps it was even a little hotter than the last time I was there, the sunsets still more resplendent. The few eucalyptus trees by the waterside had grown taller. (There had been a moment when the presence of an eucalyptus tree had been considered a protection against every tropical ill and they had been planted wherever possible.) I found again my two *malams* and, always a slow worker, I became entirely absorbed in the ever-new, ever-contradictory aspects of the Fulani language.

When my brother and Geneviève were due for leave, I felt it would be useful to compare the Fulani vocabulary I was making with words from another area. Jack Fremantle,[9] the Resident of Zaria Province, who had been a close friend of my husband, kindly offered to give me quarters and every facility.

I wish I could recall exactly how one got from Ibi to Zaria at the end of 1913. I certainly started alone down the Benue in a steel canoe, for I remember a night on a sandbank and a dark line of forest from which came, with horrible suddenness, shriek after shriek, the pitiful wailing of a child, and bursts of inhuman laughter.

Dressing for dinner was not the white man's only duty. He had also to prevent human sacrifices. It was Munshi country and the Munshi had a bad reputation for cannibalism and ritual killing. I had a revolver, the hell-man a Dane gun, the polers spears, and my two boys carried matchets. The element of surprise, the unknown sight of a white face, might achieve success. In any case, so ingrained was the sense that you were 'white man' and therefore responsible that the law should be kept that, terrified as I was, there was no hesitation. I turned back to where the crew sat happily round a fire. They were Nupe men – what did it matter to them what the Munshi did? As casually as I could, I asked the hell-man what was going on in the forest. 'Baboons,' he replied. And then I remembered that I had been told of the frighteningly human sounds baboons could make when fighting or playing among themselves. I had never heard them before, and magnified by the darkness and the surrounding stillness, it was perhaps no wonder they had deluded me.

But what I have wondered at, as an instance of animal behaviour, was the conduct of Goblin, my bush cat. 'Bush cat' was an incorrect term (should it have been caracal?), but no one could find a better one for this long-legged, small-headed, tabby-coloured creature, brought to me when only a few days old by a hunter who had killed its mother in the bush near Ibi. I was warned it could not be tamed. On the contrary, it was as affectionate and as intelligent as a dog and followed me everywhere. Yet every now and then, especially just after sundown, it would go daft, with erratic, dancing movements, twisting and turning, or leaping, goblin-like, eyes glinting, tail erect, high into the air. In those moments, obedience was forgotten; teeth and claws were sharp; and I never tried to touch it till it had tired itself out.

That night on the sandbank, it had been walking ahead of me as I strolled towards the distant forest. In the faint moonlight, I could just make out its lithe body. At the first wild shriek, we both stopped dead. As the sounds continued, Goblin backed towards me. As they reached a climax of horror, it turned and sprang on me, digging in its claws and burying its head in my neck. Its fur stood out stiffly all over its rigid body. As my arms tightened round it, for the only time in my life I felt my own hair rise on my scalp. There we stood, the two of us, the civilized and the wild, clinging to each other for comfort in the extremity of our mutual terror.

But why was the bush cat so afraid? It is true it had been reared in partly artificial surroundings, but the sounds were those of the animal world, the world to which it belonged. They were natural sounds to which it had no need to react. It was only for me, the human being, misled into thinking they had implications of human suffering, to take account of them. And why did an animal so reputedly wild, and often actually so when it was in one of its fierce twilight moods, turn to a human being for safety? It would have been understandable if it had raced away to seek shelter in the tussocks of grass or even in the canoe where it was usually fed. Instead, it deliberately chose the shelter of human arms and, equally strange, I, as deliberately, had clasped it close in an irrational hope of protection. It was as if we, in the extreme emotional tension of the moment, had gone back to some prehistoric dawn, before speech, almost before thought, when there was as yet no barrier between man and beast.

Dear Goblin, who gave me so many hours of amusement and interest and taught me so much – when later I had to leave it in a strange house for a few days and it escaped to the bush, I felt I had lost a precious link with Africa, with old and secret things.

Going with the current, we made good time down to Lokoja. From there, I suppose I must have gone up the Niger to Baro – I remember a night scene of savage beauty when the river narrowed between banks of high grass on fire. The water was streaked jet black and crimson red; the sky a turmoil of burning cinders and wheeling birds; the heat and the roar were those of a fresh-stoked furnace. At Baro, I must have taken the new railway to Zaria and Kano, via Minna. Temperamental bridges and embankments made night travel still unsafe. The train stopped for the night at Minna and, once again, I recall a night scene, though this time it was a damp and chilly one. On the train was a gang of prisoners, in the charge of a couple of warders. They were conveying boxes of specie and loads of dynamite. As I was the only European on the train, I was put in charge. (Delegation of authority was a simple thing in those days.) There were no carriages as yet on the trains. Europeans travelled in goods wagons with their camp kit and provisions. It was really quite comfortable since the wide doors stood open and, slow as was the train, there was always a breeze. The African passengers travelled in open trucks and so did the prisoners and their guards.

It was already dusk when we arrived at Minna, apparently barren of life. It was raining and cold. I had the goods wagon in which to sleep, the prisoners had nothing. It was inhuman to refuse their request for a fire around which they could stretch themselves, yet here was at once a fox-and-goose problem. How dispose of gold, prisoners, and dynamite so that the fire should not blow up the dynamite and the prisoners should not steal the gold? The warders had trailed away into the darkness. I put the gold round the fire, the prisoners round the gold, and the dynamite round the prisoners. Next morning, to my relief, all three were still there, the warders came back, a fresh lot of wood was thrust into the engine, and we trundled shakily away to Zaria.

Before going to my quarters in the European cantonment, I spent two nights with Ethel Miller, the sister of Dr Walter Miller,[10] the Hausa scholar and first translator of the Bible into Hausa. They lived then in Zaria town, in two small houses at no great distance from each other. What an astonishing couple they were – and what an astonishing woman was Ethel Miller. Much as I admired her brother's outstanding courage and life of abnegation, I could never really like him. I think he was quite often unjust to his compatriots, nor did his approach to Islam seem to me to be the right one. His sister had perhaps more uncertainties in her outlook, a few more queries to make about life. We disagreed on a hundred points but always converged again and I am grateful to think that she gave me the honour of her friendship – such a delightful, erratic, exhilarating friendship – till her death in England in 1964.

I have never been back to Zaria. Recent photographs do not show it as very different from what I remember: a gay and graceful town of palms and trees and wide spaces, enclosed, in my time, by high, bright red walls pierced with massive gates. The European cantonment was small and featureless, though it already possessed its racecourse. The Residency itself must have had some special feature since it struck me as so pleasant – though it may have been only Jack Fremantle's warm personality that transformed it and gave it the feel of a wide-open English country house on a summer's day. One could almost smell the bowls of pot-pourri and see the silver-framed photographs and the rose-covered chintzes. . . . He was much on tour and I saw little of him, but one day came a hurried note. A French Colonel of the *Infanterie Coloniale*, invalided from, I think, Zinder in the French colony of Niger and accompanied by a young lieutenant, were coming through by train on their way to Lagos to catch the French mailboat. Would I come to lunch and help entertain them?

I dressed as correctly as I could. By some trick of memory, I still see the dress I wore: a rough white material, a long skirt reaching almost to the ground, a high, whaleboned lace collar, long, almost leg-of-mutton sleeves, white shoes, white silk stockings, and a sun-helmet wound round with grey chiffon.

The two French officers kept looking at me. Then the Colonel, his tired blue eyes alight with curiosity, drew me aside: 'You are all alone here?' I nodded. 'You are here just to study a language?' Again I agreed. His voice sank. 'Our host tells me – and I believe him – that you are an honest woman – *une femme honnête*. You Englishwomen, you are incredible, but incredible!' All through lunch, he continued to meditate on the incredibility of a woman being able to live without scandal in this remote world of men. But when we parted – how ill and frail he looked – his smile was one of friendliest comprehension.

Old friends, Hanns and Isabelle Vischer (later to be Sir Hanns and Lady Vischer)[11] were in Kano and asked me to stay. They met me at the train with a four-wheeled American buggy, a coach-horn, and a pair of prancing ponies. All the way to *Gidan Dan Hausa*★ we whirled through clouds of dust, scattering crowds and flocks with blasts of the horn or lusty songs in German-Swiss. Everyone saluted 'Dan Hausa' with smiles and blessings; he and Isabelle seemed to know half the population and their compound was never without a few squatting figures waiting respectfully and patiently for the chance of speech.

Later in the day, we rode down into Kano City. I went humbly, thinking of Heinrich Barth,[12] trying to see the walls – they were still colossal, like cliffs not made by man – as he had seen them; recognizing gates, buildings, the market, dye pits, that he had described; marvelling that his dead words should have conveyed so living a picture. Nothing could have changed very much since his day; no one could better his descriptions of jostling crowds, strange faces, heaped merchandise, laden camels. In recent years, I have always refused to go into the City, wishing to keep my own fabulous memory of it. Only once was it difficult to make an excuse. Of course the City was cleaner, tidier, with some good new buildings, water, electricity, a high new resplendent mosque. But all the salt and savour had gone out of it.

Hanns Vischer – my family always called him 'Swissie' since by birth he was of a staunch Basle family – was then Director of

---

★Literally: the house of the son of the Hausa (MC's note).

Education for Northern Nigeria. No better one could have been found. He had already captured the imagination by his journey across the Sahara, following the caravan route from Tripoli in the tradition of the first explorers. Not only was he a remarkable linguist, he had an amazing talent for getting into other people's skins, for guessing what would be their hesitancies and their acceptances. He moved among the Africans with simplicity and ease, with an equal gift for laughter and for the quiet formality the older Hausa loved. His wife was equally at home among the women. Together they had fashioned a light and supple bridge between themselves and the people, made rather of liking, enjoyment, mutual respect, than the often ponderous camaraderie of today.

Unlike the South, the North did not hunger for Western education. The beginnings were slow but the foundations were solid – Katsina College[13] gave perhaps the best education the North could have had – and, on the whole, have stood up well to the immense weight put upon them in recent years by the sudden spread of schools and colleges. Girls' education was hardly thought of. The only Mission education, apart from Dr Walter Miller's few pupils in Zaria, was given by the Sudan United Mission and the Sudan Interior Mission in predominantly pagan areas.

Every visitor to Kano is shown *Gidan Dan Hausa*, now a national monument. I knew it when it was first built, its walls fresh rubbed, its domed ceilings rich with intricate designs. Isabelle Vischer had gathered together the finest Kano cloth and mats and leather-work so that there was not a jarring note in the shadowy rooms, cool and still like pools of water after the violence of the daylight. We slept on the flat roofs, the mud still warm from the heat of the day, and breakfasted in the garden under the high trees, in a dapple of sunlight and shade. The ponies stamped in their stables; the servants bustled eagerly to and fro; Isabelle gave her orders like a châtelaine administering a well-trained household. Though Geneviève Ruxton had done all she could with that impersonal Ibi bungalow, this was the first *home* I had seen, an intelligent creation based on the country's own riches, belonging to it, issuing out of it, and at the same time harmonizing with our own ideas of simple comfort, order and cleanliness.

I left it regretfully, picked up my loads at Zaria and took the train down to Jebba. The bridge was not yet built. The train crossed on a steam ferry, an unwieldy monster, looking as devil-ridden as the Juju Rock itself. The Captain was a white man, lonely and despondent. His colleague on the ferry had just died of malaria; all the company he had was a canary. He had not spoken to a white woman for months. 'Yes, some have been on the ferry. But they were too grand to speak to the likes of me.' He told me of sailing days, in and out of West Indian islands. His eyes saw them. 'Lovely, all green – the palm trees came down to the edge of the sea – little white sandy beaches, springs of clear water. We used to land there to take water and to pick up coconuts – ripe ones – as many as we could carry.' The vision of green shade, white sands and clear bubbling springs faded from his eyes as he looked disdainfully at the dun-coloured banks, the muddy, eddying water.

Nigeria does not allow herself to be tolerated: she demands either hatred or love. How sorry I was for men like these, lonely, homesick, dulled with the monotony of the hot days or shaken by a sudden death close beside them. It seemed cruel to be going home, leaving him there. I did not know then that I would not see Nigeria again for eleven years.

PART III: 1925–1931

In 1912, when Sylvia Leith-Ross was still in Nigeria working on her *Fulani Grammar*, Sir Frederick Lugard, who had for the past six years been Governor of Hong Kong, returned to the country. He was appointed Governor of Northern as well as Southern Nigeria with the express task of amalgamating them. This he did in 1914 on the eve of the First World War and presided over the destiny of the new colony until 1919.

Though technically the two British colonies were amalgamated, in practice they continued to have very much a separate existence. Each was still administered by a Lieutenant-Governor who had wide powers, while Northern District Officers were rarely appointed to the South, and vice versa. Lugard, with the personal title of Governor-General, did, however, attempt to impose Northern ideas of indirect rule on the South, with disastrous initial results in Yorubaland where the new powers of taxation given to the traditional rulers caused much resentment. Although the emirs of the North had wide powers of direct taxation before the British came, such powers were alien to the Yoruba political system.

When Lugard left he was succeeded by Sir Hugh Clifford, who left in 1925, and was in turn succeeded by Sir Graeme Thomson. It was under Thomson that Sylvia Leith-Ross's brother was appointed Lieutenant-Governor of the Southern Provinces, with his head-quarters in Lagos, next door to those of the Governor. Upton's was an unusual and, as it turned out, resented appointment. As a Northerner he had little feeling for the South, and did not mix well with his 'Southern' British colleagues. Lagos was a far cry from Muri and the emirates of the north. Already a bustling city, it had the status of a colony and all those born there were British subjects as distinct from British protected persons, the status of the vast majority of the inhabitants of the Southern Provinces. Lagos boasted a sizeable Nigerian educated élite, and women both indigenous and expatriate played a much more prominent role there than in the North. The Christian presence was very apparent, though Lagos had a large Muslim community.

The busy, cacophonous city evoked then, as now, mixed reactions from European visitors, in particular those who were accustomed to the more sedate ways of the North. And it was as a 'Northerner' that Sylvia Leith-Ross first came to live in Lagos at the age of forty-two.

★

One cannot hear oneself speak for the noise of the grinding of axes.

From a letter to the writer
from Lagos

The war years, from 1914 to 1919, were spent in French military hospitals, followed by five years of social work in London. My brother had been Resident of Bornu Province when the war broke out. He rejoined his old regiment, then went into Intelligence, and when the war ended, returned to Nigeria as Resident, Cameroons; but no thought of joining him crossed my mind. The nearly-finished manuscript of the *Fulani Grammar* had been sent to the Nigerian Government. I had received a letter saying that a Captain Taylor had also made a study of the language and asking whether I would put my own work at his disposal. Agreement seemed the only right course to take. The last personal bond with Nigeria was apparently severed. Yet a year later, without explanation, the manuscript came back with the request that I should prepare it for publication under the auspices and at the expense of the Nigerian Government. Once again, Fulani speech re-bound me to the country.

In the meantime, my brother had been appointed Lieutenant-Governor of the 'Southern Provinces' (comprising the former Southern Nigeria and a part of the Cameroons taken over from the Germans under a League of Nations mandate).[1] His headquarters were in Lagos. His wife could not join him at once and he proposed that I should come out to him for a few months.

This was a very different Nigeria to the one I had known. Indeed, it was the first time I had landed at Lagos, save for a few brief moments on my way to Forcados on a previous trip. I was perhaps never a wholehearted admirer of Sir Frederick Lugard, so I recall all the more gladly how, on that earlier occasion in 1913, this busy man had taken the trouble to think of a shy young woman, and to send a message on board the Elder Dempster mailboat, asking me to tea. One of the many immacu-

late ADCs I have met escorted me across the tumultuous bar
that guards the Lagos Lagoon to Government House on the
Marina. Sir Frederick, small, thin, his clothes hanging loosely
upon him, only his glance showing the power that was in him,
gave me tea in the big room on the first floor of Government
House. We sat amid dark Victorian furniture, in front of a large
brown teapot and the traditional tin of 'Rich Mixed' set out on a
black japanned teatray. He had never needed outward trappings
to uphold his position nor his authority. But that was in 1913.
Now we were in 1925, and Sir Graeme Thomson[2] had been
Governor since September of that year, in succession to Sir
Hugh Clifford.[3]

The Lieutenant-Governor's house was that rather gloomy
and ramshackle one-storeyed bungalow which stood, up until the
'fifties, at the corner of Force Road and the Marina. But whatever its drawbacks, enhanced by the nightly clankings of the
Sanitary Train,[4] it was infinitely preferable to exile in Ikoyi,
already a garden suburb, with its segregation from the smallest
contact with the African life which it was the officials' duty and
interest to know. Also, there was now the newly-built harbour:
every now and then the tips of masts could be seen gliding
through the branches of the tall eucalyptus trees on the Marina,
and when the port tug forced her powerful way to a waiting ship,
the whole house rocked with the swell. The sea was there, a reminder of the wider world beyond the steaming hothouse in
which we lived.

I can give only a very incomplete picture of Lagos in those
days. Apart from official dinners, the refreshing sight of men in
from the Provinces for consultation with the Lieutenant-
Governor, the occasional meetings with personal friends, or
missionaries and teachers, social life passed us by. The fact that
Lagos, as well as being the headquarters of the Lieutenant-
Governor of the Southern Provinces together with his Secretariat, was also the headquarters of Nigeria with H.E. the
Governor in residence and a Nigerian Secretariat, made for an
awkward and confusing situation.

My brother worked hard amid the conflicting problems of
East and West, Lagos and Colony, seated on the verandah at a
large wooden table heaped with files, an open umbrella poised
above his head, since the ancient roofing was no longer water-

tight. His confidential secretary, Mr Pereira, sat in a little cubby-hole downstairs, faithfully typing away at any hour of the day or night. What good men they were, many of those early Sierra Leoneans or Afro-Brazilians,[5] and what a rewarding study their life histories would make.

Although no one could accuse the Government of wasting money on European officials' housing, yet not much had been done to improve Lagos town. The slums, especially those near Carter Bridge, were of indescribable squalor; the central trading area was a rabbit warren of shanties and rickety wooden 'upstairs'; the markets were awash with mud and garbage. Yet it was easier to blame than to find a remedy, since the problem demanded a large staff, knowledge of town-planning on sites as difficult as that of Lagos Island, and a great deal of money, none of which was available. Nevertheless, the African population seemed cheerful enough and Lagos was still free from the many social problems which confront it today. Only the file labelled 'Child Hawkers' lay already on the LG's desk, growing heavier day by day.[6] Probably it has been closed at last, but it was one I was to see again and again all down the long years. Its rival in size, labelled 'Disposal of Nightsoil', is, I am sure, still open.

As far as European commodities were concerned, the United Africa Company had not yet built its emporium of plate glass, lifts and deep freeze. The firms had kept their old 'factory' look and one did not go shopping, one went 'to the canteens'. John Holt, Paterson Zochonis, G. B. Ollivant and many others were of course already there as well as some smaller Syrian firms. I do not actually remember any Indian ones, though I may be mistaken. We dealt chiefly with the Compagnie Française de l'Afrique Occidentale, where polite and pallid youths flitted about in dark and ancient quarters. It still kept the monopoly of excellent French merchandise, as also the romantic legend that its employees were all young delinquents shipped out from France to be reformed by this semi-penitentiary existence!

I have only faint memories of Ikoyi, already trim and well laid out, and as lifeless as the large cemetery one could not avoid passing four times a day on the way to or from the offices. After the masculine North, the presence of so many expatriate women – there were no children yet – came to me as a surprise. It was all to the good: houses, gardens, food – and therefore health – improved, yet their coming brought in a new element. Marooned all day in their impersonal PWD houses, without means of transport (it was some five miles to Lagos), with few household duties and little interest in the country, it was no wonder that, after a long, hot, empty day, these young wives claimed a husband's full attention when he returned from work, and looked upon it as their right to be considered and amused. Perforce, the pattern of a man's life changed: the job was no longer the centre; he was no longer single-minded. An unofficial meeting was put off because he had promised his wife to play tennis; a report was not written that evening because she had arranged a bridge party. He hoped he would not be posted to an unhealthy or isolated station; he was no longer so keen on doing much touring.

The wives themselves, with time so heavy on their hands, fell prey to small rancours, small jealousies, the desire to go one better than their neighbours. It has been said that the appearance of the first silver coffee-pot changed the face of Nigeria. In a way this was true. In the very early days, wives such as the gallant Mrs Larymore,[7] Geneviève Ruxton, Isabelle Vischer (to name only those of Government officials in the North) had led what might truly be called a pioneer life which only their wit and courage, their shared interest in their husbands' work, their belief in its value, had made tolerable for a woman. Now the life had softened, especially in the longer-occupied South. In Lagos and Ikoyi, it had become almost luxurious – and increasingly expensive. Mrs X's first silver coffee-pot caused Mrs Y to send for a silver salver, which had to be outdone by Mrs Z with a silver tray. Parties became more elaborate; more time and money had to be spent at the Club; a hundred and one small items swelled the household accounts. Promotion to a higher salary, the obtaining of an additional increment or increased duty pay became, in many cases, a pressing need. Up till then, Nigeria and the job had come first because they had had no rivals. Now a man had to think: how can I get better pay? how can I make my wife more comfortable? The silver coffee-pot had done its work.

No wives had jobs – that was not to come till the next war – and there were no women in Government service except the Nursing Sisters and the first woman Medical Officer, Dr H. S. Keer, cynical and kind, battling with the pregnant crowds at the newly-opened Massey Street Dispensary.

When I came to stay in Lagos the Yaba estate was as yet a blueprint, save for one recently finished specimen house. Duly inspected by the Lieutenant-Governor, it stood stiff and forlorn in a sandy waste. No imagination could have conjured up the swirling Yaba of today.

As for Apapa, when I look at the wharves, sheds, rails, stores, villas, the whole prodigious spread of 'civilization', it is only by a conscious effort of memory that I can recall that in 1925 Apapa was little more than a vast mudbank. A section of roadway was being built, black slime and stagnant pools on either side. As the car nosed carefully along it, the roadway trembled slightly. When the car stopped, strange plops and suckings and gurglings were heard; small crabs clambered among the mangrove roots; the smell of rot and decay hung heavy over the formless scene. Apapa is now taken for granted as the proper home of industry and commerce, as the new residential area of cement and chromium, bright paint and shiny cars. I wish a corner of the old swamp could have been left, for remembrance.

In the European society, there were more class distinctions, to use rather too heavy a term, than there are now. As far as Government officials were concerned, there were still the unfortunate Class A and Class B labels; Commerce and Government seldom mixed except officially; the Missions kept aloof from both. These three sections represented practically the whole of European society throughout the country.

Socially, Africans and Europeans did not often meet – not as often as they should have done – but how little one remembers any talk of a colour bar. People simply led different lives, at a different tempo, and with different interests. When they did meet, it was perhaps with less strain than in these more self-conscious days. They met when work or some special occasion demanded it, with ease, yet with that slight formality which may perhaps be a surer safeguard of good relations than all the mutual back-slappings and Christian names of today. I think it was Selwyn (later Sir Selwyn) Grier[8] who started – or perhaps restarted – the Lagos Cricket Club. How often, in later noisier and angrier days, have I remembered the cricket pitch at one end of the Race Course, the African players' immaculate flannels, the white men's quiet, friendly smiles and handshakes, the almost stately game, Gentlemen v. Gentlemen. . . .

Dr Henry Carr[9] was always a welcome guest and counsellor. Later, he was to be much criticized by fellow-Africans for being a tool of the British, a 'yes-man'. From what I had known of him, he only said 'yes' to what, in British thought or practice, he considered right. That he said 'yes' more often than, say, Herbert Macaulay[10] (whom my brother much enjoyed), was not through servility, but through an integrity of judgement which compelled him to see that, in some instances, the British view was the wiser one. To me, he has always stood as an example of an admirable fusion of African and European intellect, without the great driving force of a Dr Aggrey,[11] but equal to him in sanity. And what perfect English he spoke and wrote!

Bishop Oluwole,[12] large, benign and shrewd, would come to dinner, so unassuming that maybe I was not wrong in thinking that his wife's sleeves were extravagantly puffed out so as to make up for her husband's modest show of lawn. They, and Sir Kitoyi and Lady Ajasa,[13] were of the old school, at once representatives of the old school of Yoruba aristocratic tradition and of a Victorianism which they had learnt from the early missionaries. How smoothly the two blended, both in their narrowness and conventionality and in their uprightness and sense of duty.

Theirs, and ours, was too narrow a world, filled with innumerable calls to immediate duties buzzing in ears that should have been strained to catch the first sounds of political unrest, and blinding eyes that should have looked further into the future. The 1914 war had left no very obvious traces on the country, yet there were already, even in the eyes of simple men, faint cracks in the façade of British prestige. After years of being told that intertribal wars were wrong and that whoever broke the peace would be punished, it seemed strange that the British themselves should have gone to war against fellow white men. Did they teach to others what they did not practise themselves? There was an indefinite but general change of attitude. Even those like myself who had nothing to do with politics, could feel the stirring of ambition, a greater mental activity, an insistent demand for more and more education leading to greater and greater opportunities.

Indeed, the demand had become so insistent and widespread that it was time that the whole machinery of education throughout the Southern Provinces should be reconsidered. Much of it was in the hands of the Missions who had been the first in the educational field. The Education Department had issued an Education Code for their use, but it was out of date and did not take into account changing conditions and the increase in number of staff and pupils.

The Director of Education for the Southern Provinces was Selwyn Grier, whose career till then had been in the Administrative Service. His knowledge of the country and of the people was more valuable at that time than solely academic qualifications or a purely Western experience. Had he continued longer as Director, one cannot help thinking that his broader outlook, unshackled by conventional Western ideas, would have spared Nigerian children years of learning the height of the Chilterns, the Queens of England, and poems concerning primroses and Father Christmas' reindeer.

He came often to my brother's house, and when he asked me to join the Education Department as the first woman member, my profound wish to serve the country and the pleasure of working under a man so worthy of confidence, overcame my misgivings as to my abilities. A Board of Education, with Grier as Chairman, was being formed, to which I was appointed Secretary in 1926. The meetings were held in a large room lent by King's College.[14] The members were drawn from the Education Department and from the various Missions throughout the South. They eyed each other with suspicion or chilly disapproval, till the Chairman's friendly warmth and patient courtesy broke down the barriers and made fruitful discussion possible. But even so, it was curious to note how seldom any member spoke out, how little attentive thought had apparently been given to aims and means. To a newcomer like myself, it all seemed rather negative, and the picture of the child, pupil, student, was lost in a welter of rules and regulations concerning teachers' salaries, grants to Missions, the status of catechists, the role of pupil teachers, sanctions, dismissals, suspensions, building requirements, travelling expenses, veiled rivalry between Missions over the opening of new schools. There was every excuse: the demand for schools was so great, the available European supervisory staff was so small; Government and Mission funds alike were at such a low ebb that perhaps it was no wonder material problems took up the time that should have been given to wider, more informed, further-seeing thought.

The education of girls was put down regularly on the agenda, but the members' time was up long before this item was ever reached. Nevertheless, Queen's College was opened in 1927, the first Government secondary school for girls. It started in the old Hussey Memorial buildings near the Race Course. Cream-coloured, the long, low, arcaded buildings around a dusty square were a heritage from earlier days. Miss Rebecca Hussey, a pious Englishwoman, grieving over sad tales from the Coast, had bequeathed enough money to establish a cooper's workshop where Nigerian lads were taught how to make barrels for the palm-oil trade with England. Though long empty and uncared for, the buildings still held something of Victorian assurance and repose. They exist no more and Queen's College has emigrated and expanded into two homes.

When I was in England on leave, Mr Grier asked me to find a Principal for the College. There were few applicants for such an experimental post and none seemed suitable until Faith Words-worth (later Mrs Tolfree) came to see me. Daughter of a Bishop, great-niece of a poet, niece of the late Principal of an Oxford College, she was the embodiment of all that the most exacting African parent could require. And withal, the most lovable colleague and friend, with the charm of a very good child. Maybe, with all her gifts and a good deal of experience, she was not quite mature enough to know how to give shape to her educational ideals in this new environment, nor how to translate her wider conception of learning into an idiom that African parents and students could understand. I lost any close touch with Queen's College when Faith resigned, and after her sudden death I knew even less. It was only a few years ago, meeting the then Principal of the Lagos branch of Queen's, that I felt the spirit of Faith beside me, content to see that much of what she had hoped to do had at last been accomplished.

In the meantime, to everyone's regret, Mr Grier was promoted to The Gambia and for me the succeeding four years were a story of failures and disappointments not worth recording.

During the first years, I was sent on tours of inspection throughout the Southern Provinces. If the Mission schools wished to qualify for a Government grant they were obliged to

conform to its Education Code. The words 'Eleanor of Aqui-
taine' written large on a blackboard in a primary shool somewhere among the Yoruba – was it at Fiditi? – stared at by twenty
or thirty small and puzzled children, blurred my vision of the
value of education for a long time. On the other hand, that
teacher of genius, Sister Magdalen, had created an oasis of
harmony and commonsense at St Joseph's School in Calabar.
Both Education and Administrative Officers alike were unani-
mous in their praise, yet her Montessori methods were not followed elsewhere, nor (though with the general shortage of
money this was perhaps no one's fault) did she receive any extra
grant towards her work in the training of teachers, the greatest
need of the moment. Later, I was transferred to the Education
Department of the Northern Provinces. Unfortunately, Hanns
Vischer had a Colonial Office appointment and was no longer
Director of Education. I was posted to Ilorin to report on the
possibility of starting education among Muslim girls;[15] then to
Kano to open a small experimental school. Some of my ideas
may have been sound since they were approved of by the
Administrative Officers who knew the country – and any
pioneer work amongst a Muslim population had still to be
approached with care – but paradoxically it was my own Department which knew little of the African background that
turned them down.

Invalided out in 1931, I can recall the happiness of cordial and
lasting relations with all the Missions; the honour of the confidence of people like H. B. Hermon-Hodge[16] who was Resident
at Ilorin, of Gordon (later Sir Gordon) Lethem[17] and his wife, of
Hanns Vischer whose ribald letters had the trick of bringing
laughter at the very moment when discouragement was deepest.
And above all, I can recall the children. Yagbe crinkling her
nose and Mairu with her face flashing with life and intelligence
and Baraki running towards me, splendidly clothed in one string
of beads.

PART IV: 1934–1937

While Sylvia Leith-Ross was serving in the Education Department in Kano in 1929, major riots had broken out among women in south-eastern Nigeria. These had severely shaken the colonial government. They were triggered off by a rumour – unfounded as it turned out – that the colonial government was about to impose direct taxation on all adult women. The riots began in Aba and Owerri, but soon spread as far as Calabar and Opobo. In Opobo the rioters were so ferocious that the police opened fire on the crowd, killing thirty-two people and wounding a further thirty-one.

Curiously, it was Sylvia Leith-Ross's own brother, Upton Fitzherbert Ruxton, who as Lieutenant-Governor of the Southern Provinces of Nigeria in 1929 was responsible for introducing indirect rule in the guise of the Native Revenue Ordinance into the southeastern provinces, thereby triggering off the riots. Though a 'Northerner', when he took up office in the South he succeeded, in the words of Jeremy White, 'in preserving an independence of judgement which surprised his former colleagues and earned him the reputation of being "non-co-operative".'* Thus he foresaw that there would be difficulties in introducing direct taxation based on assessment of income in these provinces where the inhabitants had no tradition of direct taxation and where the chiefs seldom had any traditional authority but were appointed by government and rarely enjoyed the confidence of the people. He therefore suggested the introduction of a poll-tax instead of a tax based on an assessment of income. Even when he had been persuaded to withdraw this proposal in favour of the full application of the Native Revenue Ordinance as applied throughout

* Jeremy White, *Central Administration in Nigeria 1914–1948: The Problem of Polarity*, Dublin and London, 1981, p. 159. The account given here of Ruxton's role in the introduction of 'indirect rule' in the south-eastern provinces is based on White, pp. 160ff.

the rest of Nigeria, he asked that he be given the power to suspend assessment and levy a capitation tax instead. He also asked for additional staff in case of disturbances, which he rightly foresaw might be the consequence of assessment for direct taxation. The right to suspend direct taxation was, however, refused. Although the Governor had said in Legislative Council that the rejection of a poll-tax in favour of an income tax did not mean that income of individuals would be assessed but rather that a flat rate would be levied, varying from district to district, Ruxton assumed that a true income tax was now to be introduced. The resulting assessment triggered off all sorts of rumours about the government's intentions, and led to the disturbances Ruxton had so rightly feared might be the consequence of this policy.

In the aftermath of the Commission of Enquiry into the riots, on which sat two African barristers, Sir Kitoye Ajasa and Mr Eric Moore, the colonial government set about reorganizing native administration in the area. The Commission had been particularly critical of the way native administration had been conducted hitherto. They were critical of the powers given to chiefs appointed by Government warrant among peoples who traditionally did not invest executive authority in one individual. These warrant chiefs had in many cases become oppressive of their 'subjects' and abused the powers given to them by the government. The colonial administration, now headed by Sir Donald Cameron, whose experiences as Governor of Tanganyika had led him to believe that pre-colonial African government was essentially 'conciliar', set about discovering what the traditional institutions of the peoples of south-eastern Nigeria actually were, so that they could use these as the basis for local administration. To do this, they commissioned a number of anthropological surveys. It was in the context of this urgent concern with the 'anthropology' of the peoples administered by the British and the continued search for the underlying causes of these riots that Sylvia Leith-Ross, now in her early fifties, came out to Nigeria in 1934 to make her study of the Ibo women who had triggered off this dramatic uprising against the colonial authorities.

★

You are only an amateur? That's no matter so long as you are sincere.

Professor C. G. Seligman
to the writer

The last four years with the Education Department had made me feel so useless that it was only under constant pressure from two friends that in 1934 I applied with diffidence, and even with reluctance, for a Leverhulme Research Fellowship. To my surprise it was immediately awarded. Margaret M. Green, later to be Senior Lecturer in West African Languages and Cultures and author of *Ibo Village Affairs*,[1] had been with me for one tour in the North while I was in the Education Department, and had given invaluable voluntary help in the first small school for girls I had opened in Kano. On her return to England she had taken a Diploma in Anthropology and was given a Leverhulme Fellowship at the same time as myself.

It was not very long after the Aba Riots, or the Women's War, which had caused the Government much trouble. In spite of the lengthy Commission of Enquiry, the underlying causes of the Riots had never been fully comprehended, nor was it known whether a recurrence was likely. It was suggested that a further investigation might be useful, which would cover not only the areas directly concerned in the Riots, but also as much as possible of the general structure of Ibo life. In view of the tense situation which had been created by the Riots and of which the memory was still vivid, it was considered that women observers would create less perturbation than would men.

Margaret Green and I left for Port Harcourt towards the end of 1934. Dubious as were some of the officials as to the usefulness of our mission, and apprehensive lest some chance incident might rekindle the women's suspicions, we were yet received with that apparently inexhaustible kindness special to Nigeria, and we had permission to go where we liked.

Miss Green decided to make an intensive study of an Ibo

village group. I attempted a rather wider survey of the women in various stages of development, but once again, as when working at Fulani, I was an amateur with only a human approach to my subject. Much of the material then gathered is embodied in *African Women*,[2] still more remains in my scribbled notes, insufficiently checked to be of use save to recall scene after scene of that intense animation which constitutes Ibo life.

Miss Green settled in truly heroic discomfort in a tiny, thatched, mud-walled hut among the Abaja in the thick forest country south-west of Okigwi in what was then known as Owerri Province. I went first to the Arcadian simplicity of Eziama in the Okigwi Division, where a minute Methodist chapel gave me shelter amid hills and streams and tall forest trees. Then I moved down to the oil-palm belt, where a dense population hid itself in 'towns' like vast garden suburbs secreted in the green and breathless twilight, and again on to Port Harcourt, artificial, semi-sophisticated, with its schools and roads and electric lighting. Both Miss Green and I spent nearly all our time living directly amongst the people. Fascinating, exhausting, rare experience made up of infuriating misunderstandings and delightful incidents, of sudden frustrations and immense satisfactions, of unexpected trust and unexplained suspicion, of warm comprehension and chilly withdrawal. Whether you intended it or not, you were caught up in this exuberant Ibo life, one with the long file of women going to market, hub and centre of their lives; joining in the lamentations at the low price of palm-oil, or rejoicing as the first yam shoots appeared. You bent low over the babies and the cooking-pots and watched entranced the unique, unforgettable beauty of the women's dances. You listened to long repetitive tales of 'what he said and what she said', of dowry palaver and stories of stolen children or furious quarrels over a straying goat or a foot of farmland.

After a spell in the bush you emerged dazed, a little battered, always with a roaring sound in your ears as if you had been all but drowned in a stormy sea. A few days of silence and privacy were essential to recovery from the impact of all those voices, of those masses of human beings jostling and pressing in the dim, steaming heat of the palm belt. But how rewarding it had been:

what a wealth of new sights and sounds, what recognitions and discoveries, what sheer delight in trying to follow the intricacies of other lives, of other ways of thought. And, apart from their cupidity, which was trying, how often you felt respect for those hard-working, shrewd, vivid Ibo women and what admiration for the wisdom and tolerance and knowledge of human nature which had dictated many of their customs. It is a pity that, from the very beginning, some executive local powers had not been given them. At that time, the men would not have resented it as it would have meant little more than official recognition of powers the women already possessed. Now, too many vested interests are involved.

Men and women grumbled against Government but with no deep-seated hostility. Rather was it the old familiar grumbling of every country dweller the world over. Only in those areas which had been connected with the Aba Riots was there a jangling note of real discontent and mistrust among the women, fostered by their endless repetition of their woes, real and imagined. In other parts, the more specific criticisms were directed, rightly or wrongly, against the United Africa Company, which was the largest buyer of palm-oil and the largest seller of the cotton goods the women traders carried to the remotest markets.

At that time, eastern Nigeria was in a state of depression when palm-oil, the base of the local economic structure, had fallen in price. Often did the women question me as to the justice of the UAC raising the price of their merchandise at the same time as they lowered the price of palm-oil. In vain were they told the price of palm-oil was bound to rise and fall on the world market just as the price of yams or cassava rose and fell in their own home markets. On the other hand, did they not realize that Government, anxious to help the farmer through a bad time, had reduced the annual tax (it was as low as 3s. or 3s. 6d. in many parts), but to make up the money lost in taxation, it had to increase the import duties paid by the firms on imported goods? The firms in their turn were forced to put up their prices so as to cover these increased charges. Shrewd but egocentric, the women were not in the least convinced and as a last resort claimed: 'Would not white ladies help black ladies with this market and produce palaver? Are not all women the same?' To them it was not credible that any intelligent woman would not be a trader.

At Oguta, an important and long-established centre of the palm-oil trade, I went to see Mr Walsh, the Agent for the United Africa Company, in his office at the 'factory'. (The old term dating from earliest trading days was still used.) He told me that the day before, a deputation of twenty women had literally barred his entrance to the factory until he had listened to their grievances. He took it good-humouredly, having learnt from long experience how to deal with these Amazonian women, and indeed he was well liked by them in spite of their loud reproaches as to his meanness. 'Men and women will let you down,' he remarked philosophically but without acrimony. My cook had another opinion of these feminists – 'they no give chance for men' was his hurt comment when it came to buying fish in the market.

The most striking figure was that of the 'big' woman trader, Madam Naomi, the first Oguta woman to deal not only in palm kernels, which women had always done, but also in palm-oil. The first time I saw her was in the market which stood high above Oguta lake and from where, straight across the water, the roofs of the United Africa Company factory showed red among the palm trees. That day the market was packed with buyers and sellers; the noise was deafening, the heat suffocating. I retreated to a little mound at one end of the market and watched the throng. Suddenly it parted, as suddenly hushed. Down the wide lane strode Madam Naomi, splendid in folds of coral-pink velvet brocade, a file of women behind her and a little man in shirt-sleeves cringing beside her. She rolled slightly as she walked, waved a hand in greeting, or turned to call a sudden, imperious order. On the edge of the bank above the lake, she stopped. One arm raised, she shouted an abrupt command. There was a second's bustle on the beach below, an answering cry and, manned entirely by women, a big black canoe shot out across the lake, laden with its precious cargo of palm-oil. The quick plunging movements of the women's paddles bore it swiftly towards the further beach and the factory yard.

Naomi watched for a moment, then turned away, waved aside the little man in shirt-sleeves, pushed back her coral-pink head-tie, wiped the sweat off her brow with the back of her hand and,

1 Sylvia Ruxton at revolver practice.

2 Sylvia Ruxton in Berlin, *c*. 1900.

3 Sylvia Ruxton in 1905:
the miniature sent to Arthur Leith-Ross.

4 Sylvia Ruxton and Arthur Leith-Ross when they met in England in 1906.

5 The Leith-Ross's bungalow in Zungeru.

6 Their dogcart, the first in Nigeria.

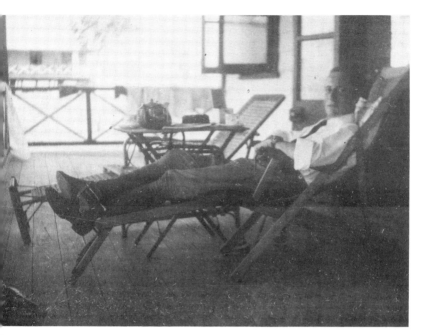

Upton Fitzherbert Ruxton as a District Officer.

Upton Fitzherbert Ruxton (left) as Lieutenant-Governor of the Southern
Provinces.

9 Sylvia Leith-Ross's house in Waterside, Onitsha.

10 Ibeze, her landlord in Onitsha

11 The rest-house where Sylvia Leith-Ross lived at the Museum at Jos.

2 Sylvia Leith-Ross at work on the pottery collection at Jos, 1962.

13 Sylvia Leith-Ross at the end of her life. (Photograph by Andrew Ganf)

leaning heavily on the shoulder of one of her women, slowly mounted the steep lane to her home, dangling a Yale latchkey as she walked.

One evening, by formal appointment, Madam Naomi came to see me in the primitive little Mission rest-house in the middle of Oguta town. Even the usual telegraphic style of my notes takes on an almost Solomon-like ring as I try to follow her description not, alas, of 'the virtuous woman whose price is above rubies' but rather of the 'rich woman' who, in Ibo eyes, is synonymous with the 'good' woman. 'She wears armlets and anklets of ivory and rolls from side to side as she walks; she strides along so that everyone may see she is a rich woman. She has innumerable children, and slaves, forty or fifty, which she pays £20 for, or more. She builds herself a house in the middle and all the slaves build their houses around her. When her cowries[3] reach too much and she needs no more slaves, she digs a pit, a deep pit, and into it her cowries are poured. When this pit is full, she seals it and digs another, and another. She buys ten wives for her son, so that all people say "He is the son of a rich woman." When Government came, it sold us gun-powder at 18*s.* a box and cloth at 12*s.* a piece which would now cost two pounds; it told us no longer to fire the mortars that sit low upon the ground and which we got from the white man in times of long ago. It told us to wear cloth, we who had gone naked, and to buy the fine things the white man had made. Then came the days when I made twenty pounds profit in a month, when I bought eight barrels of oil in a day. First in Oguta was my husband to put pan [corrugated iron] on his roof. Government told him to stop buying slaves, to build himself fine house instead. All the people were angry, they said the people who lived in the house would die. But they did not die and I built myself a house too. . . .' The portrait of the 'rich woman' was rapidly becoming a self-portrait.

At Onitsha and elsewhere, there were a number of women traders of the same calibre, but Madam Naomi, magnificently swathed in her rose-coloured velvet, sitting on a hard wooden chair, knees wide apart, sipping neat whisky, was the most dramatic of them all.

For the next months I travelled through the greater part of what was then the Owerri Province. Much of the time I dealt only with illiterate or semi-literate people, chiefly women, whose main contact with the outside world was represented by the price of palm-oil. But it is interesting to note that even when talking to men, traders, clerks or teachers, often wide-awake and intelligent men, their conversation had no political implications and such words as self-government, independence, freedom, were never heard. Trade, land tenure, Native Courts, title-taking, dowries, these were the usual subjects.

It seemed to me in bad taste to question the Africans concerning European officials, and to the credit of their own good taste, they never sought to gossip nor to criticize, nor to involve me in a discussion. Very occasionally, you could feel a certain man was heartily disliked – and their judgement was generally accurate. Occasionally, in telling of some circumstance, they might say: 'The DO made a mistake but he did not know our custom,' or 'He was unjust, yet we know his heart is good and we are not angry.' And quite often, you heard that all-covering compliment which in its terse pidgin English is perhaps the ultimate praise a man can hope for: 'He try.'

It is true that not many Administrative Officers had the time and opportunity – and sometimes even sufficient interest – to know as much of the background of their people as they should have done. Obscure questions such as that of the *osu*;[4] the dislocation of village life during the building of a *mbari* house;[5] the important role played by the womenfolk; the memories of events, already remote to us but still present to them, such as the Aro Expedition, the murder of the unfortunate Dr Stewart and its punishment,[6] and of course the more recent Women's War, were not sufficiently taken into account. On the other hand, how often when I was tentatively putting forward what appeared to be a reasonable complaint to a patient District Officer, did I find that the subject had already been thrashed out or the experiment had been made and had failed. In fact, though my heart remained in the North, I had to admit that our ancient Northern Nigerian prejudices were without foundation! Residents, District Officers, Assistant District Officers were as hard-working and as conscientious as those I had known in the North, and here in the East they had perhaps a harder task, given the difficulty of the Ibo language,[7] the density of the population and – so it appeared at first – its lack of organization.

Yet there was an uneasiness in the air to which I could not put a name. Had Nigeria sailed into the doldrums – or was it the calm before the storm – or was it just the weight of the steaming heat of the palm belt that pressed upon my spirits? No European seemed quite sure whither he was going. I remember stray thoughts passing through my mind, formless criticisms based on nothing tangible. 'They don't seem sure of themselves – they're on edge – the Women's War is long over but it shook them badly – there's too much drinking – they're untidy – Bloomsbury manners don't suit Nigeria.' There was some sort of weakness, of fatigue perhaps, which caused this slight demoralization, for I do not think that the possible insecurity of the future for all officials in the country was as yet a factor. There were political battles being fought in Lagos, but here in the provinces the repercussions were mild. The advent of ultimate independence was recognized in theory, but it still seemed a very long way off. And after all, when you had just been trying a case of child-stealing, twin murder[8] or witchcraft, political maturity might appear to you as a very distant achievement.

Even when I went down to Port Harcourt and met educated Africans of high standing, they would say: 'If we were the Government, we would do so and so . . .' but I never remember anyone in those days saying, 'When we are the Government . . .', though of course they were vocal in their criticisms of official policies. The idea – and the ideal – of independence and self-government must already have been in their minds but, except in the minds of actual politicians, I do not think it had taken any formulated shape. It was more than a dream, but it was not a pressing need. It would come in time, in a still rather dim future, and in the meantime, though the white man was often tiresome, he did not really count for very much in their own private African life.

As for the rest of the country, with no settlers,[9] no plantations, no Western industries, only small-scale tin and coal mines, there were millions who could comfortably ignore his presence save when the annual tax collection came round or too many boundary disputes or Native Court cases called for the attention of Resident or District Officer. Schools, hospitals, roads were of course multiplying, Government Department staff was increasing, commercial firms were opening more buying stations for local produce suitable for export, more wives and children enlivened the scene, yet white faces were only minute dots on the surface of that immense and crowded land.

★   ★   ★

In 1936, both Miss Green and myself were generously awarded a second Leverhulme Research Fellowship. Miss Green returned to her former headquarters at Umueke Abaja, and I went to Onitsha to study yet another section of Ibo womanhood.

After the serried palm trees of Owerri, it was good to find open country once more and to see the Niger curving between the sandbanks. Though Onitsha was still a small town compared to what it is today with its additional 'Fegge lay-out'[10] and its ribbon development of smart villas along the Onitsha–Oguta road, it was (just as it was when I first saw it in 1907), the most alive, the most bustling town I know of in Nigeria. Lagos or Ibadan had larger crowds, but the people seemed to be just walking or just sitting. In Onitsha there was purpose in every stride, determination in every gesture. Each man knew what he wanted and he was getting it, not fiercely nor angrily but with complete assuredness.

There was not much traffic on the roads, there were still shady lanes between mud walls, and quiet corners where children played in the warm dust and tranquil women pounded their yams in the wooden mortars or turned over the crimson peppers drying in the sun. Then suddenly you would come on New Market Road or on the Beach to a blinding glare, an immense clamour of voices, the clang and clash of iron oil-casks, the deep-throated *a-ah*, *a-ah*, as the labourers with rippling muscles pushed and pulled the heavy-laden trucks, the smell of palm-oil (the true, traditional smell of the Coast), the padding of innumerable naked feet and, between the old warehouses and bungalows high on their stilts (the first buildings put up by the trading firms), glimpses of the Niger, stately, steel-bright under the midday sun.

The market had not yet dreamt of terraces and stand-pipes. It stood on the same site as now, huge, always thronged and, as you could see at a glance, a 'rich' market by any standards. Indeed, it seemed as if Western goods predominated, especially enamel ware and Manchester cloth, until you came to the large space reserved for the women in from the farms bringing their yams, cassava, plaintains, oranges, peppers, and all the produce of the countryside. These women paid no market dues; the regular stall-holders could rent a cement stall for one pound a year or a plot on which to build their own stall at 5s. a year. An official estimate gave the number of stalls at 2,400, and many more could have been disposed of if more land had been available. All stall-holders were supposed to keep the surrounding space clean. My notes remark acidly: they do not.

The volume of trade must have been enormous. Some of it used the Niger, but I always wondered that the project which was spoken of in Port Harcourt (in January 1937), of a line which would link the existing railway at Aba with Onitsha, via Owerri, had not been more closely studied. Palm-oil went out by stern-wheeler; large quantities of foodstuffs came in by canoe. I was introduced to the head-woman of the fish-wives, who was also the President of the 'Co-operative of Aboh', and I listened to the recital of her and her mother's doings which had the same biblical ring as the life-story of Madam Naomi. 'My mother was the first to start a daily market for fish, both the fresh and the dried. She called the Ibologwu, the Senaga, the Idah, who are Igala people, to come. She protected the Ikede and the Ijaw. . . . But it was I who called the Jukun to trade, it was I who opened Akiri and Uchi and Aboh. . . .' At that moment, she was waging war against Asaba, which is immediately opposite Onitsha on the west bank of the Niger and which was trying to capture the fish trade by bribing the up-river people to unload their canoes there instead of Onitsha. Looking at the stern face and upright figure of Amede Odili, I had no doubt of the outcome. She had not the flamboyance of Naomi; it was her very quiet that proclaimed her strength.

From rollicking Waterside, you turned to Inland Town, silent and secret, hidden in what seemed almost a primeval forest, so thick and high and intertwined were the trees, so deep the shadows. Only one rough track led through it, fed by a maze of little paths. Even when I lived there, I could never find my way alone, nor penetrate its withdrawn, decorous life. All the 'best people' lived there; no Faubourg St Germain could have been more jealous of its traditions. Some of the younger men had built themselves houses in Waterside, but it was to show off their wealth, not to live in.

The Resident of Onitsha Province made no objection to my living alone in the native town, first in Waterside, then in Inland Town. In Waterside I was fortunate in being able to rent the first floor of a recently-built cement house – known as an 'upstairs' since it possessed a storey – in Old Market Road which was then a wide and quiet thoroughfare, yet close to the heart of the town.[11] Too close perhaps. After the previous year's strenuous times in Owerri Province, I had but to sit still and let the life seep into me. The women came readily and talked sensibly. They were more sophisticated than my friends of the Eziama and Okigwi bush, but equally lively and never suspicious as those of the Women's War areas had been. They brought up many a thorny subject themselves, such as polygamy, which many considered a better system than monogamy, since a Christian marriage might bring hardship to a wife deserted by her husband and, if a Roman Catholic, she would be forbidden to marry again. They spoke of the injustice of turning away the former wives of a polygamist who becomes a Christian; the problem of what to do with girls who have finished school and yet do not want to marry at once: 'They will not farm, they will not help their mothers in the market. All they do is to sit around or learn to sew frock' or, bored and restless, 'take to witchcraft'. And anyhow, once married, the girl's schooling is soon forgotten. If she did read, her husband would say to her: 'Was it for reading the newspaper that I married you?' Yet, paradoxically, the demand for girls' education is today insistent and often a young man will himself pay his fiancée's school fees.

Teachers came too. I cannot remember whether it was in Onitsha or Owerri that several teachers in turn came to ask why Government had banned the importation of the books of D. H. Lawrence. Was it because they had some special power in them, meaning had they power like books on astrology or 'Indian

Powder'[12] (which had also been banned) and the white man feared they would make the black man too powerful? And why was it that all Indian students seemed to pass their exams? The white men said it was not because of the powerful books or the Indian Powder and yet it seemed strange that they should pass in such numbers. Students in Nigeria corresponded with Indian students who told them they need only do as they did to pass also. These were saddening conversations, offset by others with men who were really keen on their job once you could get them away from the question of their pay, their quarters, their chances of promotion. But in nearly all of them, I found a complete ignorance of local conditions unless they actually belonged to the town or village in which they were working. The reply of an excellent and intelligent Travelling Teacher, a man from Bonny stationed in Owerri, was typical: 'I cannot say . . . (in answer to my questions on the children's general habits), I only see the scholars. . . .' Apparently after all these years, education was still unrelated to life.

My landlord was a senior clerk, an Onitsha man of good family – how 'county' these Onitshans are – who was of the greatest help in every way. Consciously and unconsciously, he allowed me an insight into the mind of a representative Nigerian, well-educated by local standards, proud of his race and his status. He was only Westernized insofar that he knew all about files and typewriters, often wore correct and well-made European clothing and had built himself this semi-European house in the 'best' part of Waterside, though he himself continued to live in the more aristocratic Inland Town which was also his parents' home. This fact alone showed how little he was de-tribalized[13] or in any way an alien among his own people. On the contrary, he was still a devoted son to his ageing parents, mingled easily Christian tenets and pagan practices, and was deeply conscious of his responsibilities towards his own people.

Often he, and others like him, deplored the fact that the Missions did not know more about African customs. If a legitimate compromise were not possible, at least a sympathetic comprehension could be shown towards the many good points in tribal rules, even if these did not coincide with Western conventions. The condemnation of dancing was what upset them most, and indeed it was profoundly regrettable that that crowning beauty of African life should have been so vilified and misunderstood.[14] Nor was there any comprehension of the bonds that held the people to their land, and blended with their worship of fertility. The first Roman Catholic missionaries had been Alsatians, often of peasant origin. The love of the earth was in them too, and they looked at a row of well-tended yams with the same eyes as their proselytes. The modern missionaries seemed so often to be town-bred: having to deal so much with the sons of the soil, it was a pity they themselves had been brought up on pavements. My landlord recognized all that the country owed the Missions in the way of education, but he had no spiritual needs that they could satisfy. Yet his thoughts were a continual mingling of seen and unseen worlds, and like so many of his compatriots, he dreamt of a 'civilization' – the hackneyed word took on a new and splendid sound – which he could not describe but which he knew to be a harmony of matter and of spirit.

He was above average in intelligence, range of thought, energy and ambition. He spoke freely about the past and the future, and analysed the faults and virtues of his people with shrewd frankness and much humour. During our long discussions he might show bewilderment at some of the ways of Government, but never actual hostility nor bitterness. He apparently accepted our presence with equanimity, and though irked occasionally by some regulation, he never for a moment gave the impression that he was chafing beneath an unbreakable yoke or was wounded in his dignity as a free man. So little was there any sign of restiveness under British rule in anything he told me about himself or others that the thought of the existing regime coming to an end except in the far future was never present to my mind, nor do I think it was present to his.

This experience, and many others like it, are difficult to reconcile with the later demagogues' passionate assertions regarding enslaved populations groaning in misery. I can only bear witness to my own small circle of personal experience, and if accused of being myself so steeped in an imperialist tradition that I was blind to the truth, I can only reply that my long friendship towards the African would have restored the balance of my judgement and rectified my distorted vision.

I cannot leave Onitsha – where he lies buried – without evoking
the image of James Stuart Young. In England, there may be still
a few who remember his name as a writer of stories and some indifferent poetry. In Nigeria, he was an unexpected figure and,
when I met him, already a shadowy one, pathetic and almost
tragic, like a bird of once brilliant plumage now near to death, all
brightness dimmed.

From what I could gather of his life (whether fact or fancy, I
do not know), he was born in Manchester of poor parents, was
educated at the local Board school, and later gained a precarious
living by writing articles for the *Manchester Guardian*. When he
was twenty-two, a doctor told him he was tubercular and
advised him to go to the West Coast of Africa. Strange advice in
those days, though perhaps the doctor thought it better to die
quickly of yellow fever on the Coast than to linger miserably in a
Manchester garret. Whatever the reason, the advice was good.
Stuart Young found a vacancy in a firm on what was then the
Gold Coast, regained his health, moved to Nigeria, and started
his own trading firm in Onitsha. He was said to have made a
small fortune during the war but did not know how to keep it.
When I knew him, he was living with a single servant in a ramshackle wooden house not far from my own 'upstairs', poor and
often ill. The few Europeans then in the station would willingly
have received him, but he was touchy and difficult and preferred the society of rather shady African lawyers among whom
he could feel superior.

He came to see me fairly often, since to talk of the past was,
for a few moments, to recapture his youth. The procedure was
always the same. His boy brought a note, written in French in a
style *respectueusement galant*, asking whether I would give him a
cup of coffee on my terrace – 'and we will talk of France'.

Precisely at nine o'clock, he arrived, tall, thin, head thrown
back in a posture of outmoded elegance. With hardly a greeting,
he joined me on the terrace overlooking the quiet road. We sat in
silence, looking at the stars. He never drank anything except innumerable cups of black coffee. When at last he lit his cigarette,
I knew the floodgates of memory would open. At some moment
in his life he had known Swinburne, Oscar Wilde, Aubrey
Beardsley, Morris, Rossetti – later Bernard Shaw. Then he spoke
of French poets and painters, of the Quartier Latin, nights on

Montmartre, dawns on *les quais*, feastings in the studios and passionate discussions with celebrated men on art and life. Possibly these tales were not always true. Perhaps they were like the coloured balloons children play with, and as he danced them up and down before my eyes – or rather before his own eyes – they lifted him for a moment above the misery of his present life. Should a cruel and incredulous hand have burst one of the gay balloons, the man himself would have collapsed.

At midnight, he stood up. Correct and courteous, he would say smilingly: 'I seem to have talked only about myself. Forgive me.' Then suddenly the bright balloons dropped to the ground. For an intolerable instant, tragedy looked out of his eyes as he saw himself as he was, the loneliness, the emptiness, and death quite close. Humbly he added: 'Thank you for having listened.' Gathering up his balloons again, lighting a last cigarette, he went away.

The last time I saw him, he was crossing the main road, head thrown back, with that peculiar walk never seen nowadays and which the Romantics called *nonchalant*. He wore a salmon pink silk shirt and white linen trousers, and carried a red harmattan lily in his hand.

A few days later, I left from Port Harcourt for home on the little *Wahehe* of the Woermann line. In the evening the German captain, the cook and the chief steward played classical music to the enrapt passengers. Innumerable canaries, kept by crew and passengers alike, fluttered in and out of saloons and cabins. Slowly the ship swung to the West Coast roll. Peacefully, I sorted out my many notes for the report to be made to the Leverhulme Trust.

PART V: 1941-1943

Although Sylvia Leith-Ross had been away from Nigeria for only four years when she came back in 1941 to assist the wartime colonial administration, the country had undergone important changes. The long-drawn-out world depression had come to an end. The main economic effects of the war in Nigeria were to stimulate local manufacture of those goods that could not be imported because of the activities of the German submarines and to increase demand for her palm-oil and tin, which could no longer be obtained by the Allies from south-east Asia as a result of the Japanese occupation of their colonies there.

Nigeria itself was bordered to the west and north by Vichy-French territory. Lagos, which served as a major port for the transhipment of materials and planes destined for the North African campaign, seemed vulnerably close to Vichy Dahomey.

Not only were the British concerned about the strategic vulnerability of their colony; they were also at pains to secure the loyalty of their colonial subjects, for the war broke out at a time of heightened political activity in Lagos, where a new generation of politicians were proving less patient and more critical of the slow pace at which the colonial government was apparently moving towards sharing power with the educated élite. There were still only four elected Nigerian representatives on the Legislative Council and not a single Nigerian on the Executive Council.

★

Suddenly the word 'Emancipation', traced in golden letters on a garnet-red poster, surged into sight and vanished again. 'The point is,' said Paul Desjardins, 'to know what that word means to these particular people.'

Daniel Halévy,
*Péguy et les Cahiers
de la Quinzaine*

In 1941, I was looking after Belgian refugees in Devonshire when I was asked to return to Lagos to help in the war effort there. Liverpool to Lagos via Halifax and Trinidad was a two-month journey on a Dutch boat, the valiant little *Amstelkerk*. Somewhere off Sierra Leone, there was a rumour that Freetown had been bombed out of existence. When we reached it, we could only wonder that it was not so. The harbour under its high green mountain resembled a large and crowded bowl of goldfish, so thick swam the ships in the oily waters, offering the perfect target.

Arrived in Lagos, I found myself attached to the Political and Economic Research Organization, generally known as PERO, with indefinite duties. For myself, I wanted to gauge the 'feel' of the country and of the common folk; to see how much impact the war made on African life, outside the Coast towns such as Lagos; and to know which of the many rumours that flew about were accepted and which were rebutted.

The Lagos hinterland, that is to say, the Yoruba country, was the most closely concerned with the war. The central seat of Government was at Lagos with all its comings and goings of ships and planes; the railway ran through a large part of it; one side of it bordered on Vichy-controlled Dahomey. It was far ahead of the North and still some way ahead of the East in education; it had had longer contact with the European than either. It was natural that public opinion would be more sensitive, would have a better grasp of world affairs and of the possible repercussions of the war on Nigeria itself. It would be more aware of the immense issues involved, even of the physical dangers to which people might be exposed.

I found this to be more or less true among the teachers, pastors, clerks in commercial firms, retired policemen or civil servants, with whom I was able to talk at length. Their views were of course egocentric and restricted by their limited knowledge. The price of yams in the local market was naturally of more immediate concern than whether bombs were falling on London. Yet there was some comprehension of the situation and at the same time a steadiness about these people, a core of sound good sense, which it was a relief to find. There were no loud protestations of loyalty to the British, but equally no flagrant advantage was taken of our plight. In spite of their increased ambitions and heightening desire for power, they – up-country at least – did not seek to make use of our difficulties to further their own ends. Physical danger was a remote thing to most of them, yet they knew it was present and neither men nor women gave any sign of hysteria, nor did I hear any recriminations that we, their nominal protectors, should have let them in for these hazards. If enemy forces had landed, I doubt whether any of these men would have fought for us or for their country, even if they had had the means, but I am sure they would have done all they could by ruse and ingenuity to save our lives. Even during some especially tense moments, I always felt certain that I could appeal to any African, and even more certainly to any African woman, for protection. And occasionally there might have been not only protection but aggression. The further you were away from civilization, the more chance there was of a little body of men slipping on to the rest-house[1] verandah in the dusk: 'If Ja'man come, white woman go tell us how we go kill 'em!' and an atavistic gleam of pleasure would cross their resolute faces. Knowing there was not a spare rifle in the country even if they had known how to use one, I shamelessly advised them to go back to their bows and arrows and to seek out the old men who knew the most lethal poisons.

As far as the economic life of the country was concerned, the war had not made itself felt to any great extent amongst the ordinary people. Not a sufficient number of men had joined the Army to make any great difference to the farming of food crops. Cash crops, however, suffered through lack of transport and shipping. I can still smell the mounds, or rather hillocks, of burning cocoa outside Ibadan, cocoa which had to be bought by the Government so that the farmer should not suffer, but which could not be marketed. The European canteens were gorged for a few days after the arrival of a ship from South Africa, then became empty caverns. Cotton goods from India replaced many of those from Manchester. In the bush, where even weaving and pottery-making had lapsed, it was taken up again. By an unfortunate omission, no steps had been taken to ensure a supply of salt for the native markets, and this caused some of the few bloodless but unnecessary disturbances in the South. The traditional salt trade from Aïr had been partially revived, but the South had become too used to the whiter, smoother imported salt to be content with the coarse salt the Tuaregs brought down to Kano, and, rightly or wrongly, the United Africa Company was blamed even more than Government. Indeed, over and over again, I was astonished to find how strong was the feeling against the Company, even much stronger than it had been in 1935 when I was in Owerri. Every conversation brought up its name in one way or another. The speakers inferred that UAC had plenty of salt but would only sell it if the customer bought some other goods at the same time. It charged inflated prices for old stocks which had been imported long before the war. It would never allow an African to start the smallest industry for fear it might compete with its own sales. Government paid the piper but it was UAC who called the tune. 'The Governor does nothing without UAC's permission.' No arguments, no evidence would induce the speakers to retract a single accusation, and these accusations were widespread, made by every category of people I met, and not only by those engaged in trade. Other firms were not attacked, though it is possible that the term 'UAC' had come to cover all European trading firms in the minds of Africans.

As for rumours, by the time they reached up-country, they had lost much of their force. The 'fact' that rich young men in England had paid large sums to the British Government so as to be given imaginary jobs in Nigeria, safe from bombs, was of little interest to the people of Oyo or Ilesha. Even the 'well-known fact' that Their Majesties the King and Queen were living in Lagos at Government House 'only taking a short walk along the Marina at night' so as not to be recognized, did not stir them. So long as their own Resident was 'on seat'[2] and their

DOs came and went amongst them, the vagaries of Royalty and rich young men did not concern them.

The 'feel' of Lagos was different. As would be expected, reactions were more violent, self-seeking more obtrusive; latent antagonism was dimly felt and the opportunity to assert political aims was too good to be missed. There were more loud protestations of loyalty than in the Provinces, yet judging from the amount of white calico acquired by the leading men, flags of surrender might have flown from many an African housetop before an enemy ship had dropped anchor. But even in Lagos, the small people would have stood by us whatever the bigger men might have done. My African driver, a resourceful lad, announced with a broad grin: 'We boy, we talk together, we savvy what we go do if Ja'man come. White man he do what we tell him. All go be well.' His plan was for all the Europeans to hide in the bush, leaving their boys behind in Lagos. When the enemy landed, the boys would come forward with many a 'Yes, Sah!' and 'Welcome, Sah!' and soon every German officer would have an apparently devoted staff around him. Then, one morning, every steward would put ground glass into every master's cup of coffee. . . . 'If soldier no get officer, he no good. White man come back from bush. War done finish.' In their feelings towards the British among the lesser folk, I think there was a certain amount of personal loyalty towards individual Europeans but an even greater love of doing the other man down by astute trickery and cleverness. They would merely be enacting with gusto one of their own familiar folk tales in which the cunning always destroyed the strong.

Maybe it was as well the people as a whole were not put to the ultimate test. It was already an inestimable boon that on the whole, we had a stable and trustful population behind us. It was also a tribute to the men who had worked so long among them, building up that stability, inspiring that trust. A certain amount of propaganda came over from Dakar via Dahomey, poor stuff which made little impression. Agents and counter-agents darted across the ill-guarded Dahomey frontier and back again, weaving such a cat's cradle of crossing and double crossing that they can no longer have known to which side they really belonged.

The Free French, all bravery and pathos, tore up and down the country with an alarming disregard for security. African troops with white officers from the Belgian Congo lived in neat camps, their neat lorries parked neatly in a corner and the black, yellow and red flag of Belgium flying above them. VIPs came and went in an eddy of Top Priorities and Top Secrecies. The few Germans and Italians in the country had been interned. The Syrian and Lebanese traders, as far as one could tell, were loyal. They gave generously to all the charitable funds and went out of their way to be helpful.

At all events, there was one of them who was not a hypocrite. I keep an unforgettable memory of a tiny enclosed garden in a native town – it may have been Oshogbo – a riot of jasmine and little pink roses, butterfly-light and tenderly innocent in the heavy African air. Tea was laid out on Turkish-looking stools, consisting of ice-cream soda, a newly opened tin of Rich Mixed biscuits and a mound of chocolate creams. My hosts were a young Syrian trader and his French-speaking wife, and the occasion for the party was my wish to be introduced to the bride's mother, reputed to be the first Syrian woman to have ventured to Nigeria. She had been ill, so the presentation took place while she was seated in a heavy armchair, swathed from head to foot in exquisite lilac silk, beringed and braceleted with gold. She sat there like an Eastern queen on a golden throne, piercing eyes above hawk-like features, incredibly old, incredibly alive. Our greetings to each other were bejewelled with compliments and sumptuous with expressions of gratitude. Suddenly she stood up, raised one clawlike hand, threw back her lilac-veiled head: 'God scatta the Ja'man! God save the Engleesh!' rang out in the tones of a prophetess of old. Did a cold wind, for an instant, stir the papers on Adolf Hitler's desk?

A little later, I saw her again, recovered from her illness and intent on business. She had for the moment laid aside her lilac silks and was clad in a ragged sort of nightshirt, felt slippers on her feet, and a worn sun-helmet poised sideways on her head. I think she was genuinely glad to see me and sent a servant flying for the inevitable ice-cream soda, but in the meantime the day's takings – they were considerable – had to be counted and I found myself sitting on the edge of the rough pavement, my feet in the gutter, counting pennies and shillings into neat piles on a wooden tray while my hostess poured forth her woes and her triumphs, interspersed with prayers for a British victory and the downfall of all our enemies.

For a time, I was lent to the Information Office which distributed some mild pro-British propaganda literature throughout the country. At a time of acute shortage of shipping space, it was distressing to find what large quantities of quite unsuitable material were sent out. Bale upon bale remained unused, and much of what was distributed, was misunderstood. What roused real anger was a coloured recruiting poster designed in England, no doubt with the best of intentions. It represented a couple of good-looking African soldiers in smart khaki uniforms but with the bright scarlet lips of a Nigger Minstrel on Brighton beach. In many minds, this was a premeditated insult. Another publication showed the totalitarian as opposed to the democratic way of life. To European readers, the pictures were telling and convincing. Alas, the Nigerian also found them telling, but the wrong way round. Confronted with a photograph of ranks of Italian children in stiff military uniforms, complete with rifles, standing at attention beneath a large portrait of Mussolini, they gasped with admiration, and turned with scorn to the opposite page on which some cheerful but rather ragged Boy Scouts were boiling a tin kettle over a fire of twigs. A dramatic photograph of an old French couple cowering behind a hedge, all their belongings tied to an ancient bicycle, while a squad of German soldiers marched up the road, brought forth shouts of laughter. 'They have stolen the bicycle and now the police are going to catch them!' Bundles of articles were sent out on the strangest subjects such as the war-time midday concerts at the National Gallery, Italian opera, and 'The Passing of the Messenger Boy.'

I do not remember a single item which aroused more than a moment's interest except perhaps pamphlets giving statistics of the size and number of British ships or planes or guns or bombs. The effort required to produce these numbers was of course not appreciated, but the long rows of figures were more impressive than all our well-meant exhortations to 'Fight for Freedom' or 'Defend Democracy'.

It was no easy thing to know what form, if any, legitimate

propaganda should take. Even those closest to the African could seldom guess how their minds would work, to what sentiment or emotion or motive one could appeal, what would arouse their admiration, their resentment or their mockery. Take for example the appreciation of 'success stories'. When the success was exemplified by the attainment of riches and position, or a quick deal at the expense of another, or a cunning way out of a difficulty, the audience was delighted and followed every move. When the success was of a more subtle, immaterial kind, it called forth no response save a certain bewilderment as to what the white man saw in the story. This trait was especially noticeable when dealing with tales of heroic acts which were intended to stir the readers to emulation or to admiration of the British character. Often I myself was deeply moved by these stories of shipwrecked crews, of men laying down their lives for others, not only because they were my own countrymen doing these brave things but because their individual acts ennobled humanity at large, since spirit so transcended matter. But my audience could see nothing save a dismal and rather dull tale of failure. It was not so much that they could not represent to themselves any accurate picture of the scene and the actors, it was the fact that they could not grasp there could be victory except in terms of a material triumph. I would say: 'How brave of that boy to rush into the fire to save a child!' They would reply: 'But what good did it do him? – he was burned to death himself.' Or they would read of men working their guns till all were killed or wounded. 'They would have done better to surrender at once' was all the comment. Heroism or endurance or sacrifice in itself was not enough, it must have a successful outcome. Is it perhaps a very English characteristic to be indifferent to success or failure, to be as proud of, say, the Dunkirk retreat as of any victory? to be more pleased to travel than to arrive?

Other aspects of my work were troubling. Every war must offer the same problem: how win the present war without endangering the future peace? It was all very well for those who were in Nigeria only 'for the duration'. Their job was to win the war and that was all there was in it. Those who would remain behind agreed that victory was the first imperative, yet watched many of the happenings with dismay, knowing it was they who would have to pick up the pieces.

Till then, and in spite of the 1914 war which had never really come very close to Nigeria, the mass of the people still thought of the white race as one, united by colour, education, religion. History books should have taught them otherwise, but history seemed usually to stop at the Wars of the Roses. They thought of the white men as being 'brothers', with all the implications connoted in the African mind by that term, bound to assist each other and having the same aims and interests. All these white men were rich, and had come into the world with ready-made knowledge and skills. Therefore, for the time being, they dominated the African. It was up to the African to get what he could out of the white man in the way of education and 'savvy', so that eventually he could attain the same status. In the meantime, he felt no great animosity towards his white masters unless they interfered too much in his private affairs, and he still felt an admiration, almost an awe, for their power and wealth and knowledge and their air of authority.

After all, in the first days, it was solely by prestige, only occasionally backed by rifles, and not many of those, that the handful of white men had controlled the vast country. To a certain extent, they had been controlling it ever since by the remains of that prestige. Now the last remnant was vanishing – had indeed vanished.

Every time we indicted Germany or Vichy France, we indicted ourselves as well. Except for the travelled or highly educated few, Europeans had been a mass conception for so long that whatever cruelty or treachery or injustice we attributed to our enemies was seen as a possible attribute of ourselves. Supposing our anti-Vichy propaganda were successful, and a real hatred of French domination were aroused, we could not be sure where that hatred would stop. 'Frenchman' could easily turn into 'European', which would include 'British'. Even sabotage, once learned, might become a dangerously indiscriminate habit.

Further, outside and apart from our own propaganda directed against a section of fellow-Europeans, another and even more radical change, noticed by few, was taking place in the black-white attitude of the masses. Perhaps for the first time, except in individual cases, an element of contempt had crept into their minds: these 'civilized' white men could nevertheless kill each other in great numbers, their rich towns could be destroyed, their expensive homes burnt down, they could be tortured and starved, they could cringe and beg for help and for money. And, curious sidelight emerging from conversations with observant Africans who had been in contact with our troops or sailors, for the first time in their lives these Africans had met a number of Europeans *less educated than themselves.* Especially in Nigeria, where education – even though primarily regarded in its materialistic form – is rated so highly, this failure to attain a higher standard, or at least an equal standard to their own, came as a shock. They had always taken it for granted that all Europeans were educated men. Had we not prated of our universal compulsory education system, our magnificent schools and colleges? Yet here were grown men whose English was more limited, less grammatical, worse pronounced than their own, men who never seemed to read anything except a newspaper and who were more ignorant of history or geography than themselves. In their conversations with me, the speakers took pains to be tactful. They spoke tentatively so as not to hurt my feelings: 'We thought all Europeans were educated. . . ?' They were careful to show no disdain, only sheer amazement that they should have been mistaken. You could not help feeling that this discovery was perhaps the final insidious blow which shattered the crumbling edifice of white superiority.

I made no notes while in Nigeria during the war, but I find a rough 'Résumé of informal conversations with Government officials, missionaries, and all classes of Africans, mostly belonging to the Western Province', which may be of interest as coming from someone not belonging to any special circle. I must have written it some time in 1942.

The spirit of Nigeria is not good. The educated and semi-educated African is becoming, inevitably, more aware of himself, more grasping after material, social, and economic advantages. He is more vocal – in England through white sympathizers; and more aggressive – in Nigeria through strikes and go-slow policies.

As far as the war is concerned, time and energy on the part of Government are wasted settling an infinity of small disputes; African labour, clerical or manual, has not got its mind on the job; the African farmer is discontented with the price of the produce he wants to sell and with the lack of imported goods he wants to buy, and suspects the hidden hand of combines behind both these phenomena.[3]

The general impression gained from listening to much spontaneous talk is that the African would respond better to present war demands if he could count on a more promising future. Leaving aside extremist political demands such as self-government (brought into sudden prominence by Indian events), there is a widespread demand for post-war economic and industrial expansion which would benefit the African himself and give him room to develop. The war has already created some local industries. Will these be allowed to continue after the war? Will security and perhaps some capital and training be obtainable for such Africans as wish to start other industries? The African discusses these points with good sense and restraint but the conversation invariably ends with the assertion: 'Government will not allow us.' When this assertion is queried, he adds: 'UAC will ask Government not to allow us and Government will have to obey.' That HM's Government is under the thumb of the UAC is believed by all and no argument will shake this belief. Even an illiterate smith, far out in the bush, when asked why he did not make more matchets or simple tools, replied: 'What is the good? UAC would forbid my selling them. They want to be the only people to sell anything.' This point of view may be exaggerated, but the fact remains that the fear and dislike of this great combine does hamper the country's healthy development; and the assumption that the Nigerian Government is the servant of trade interests undermines its prestige even in loyal minds.

The Nigerian people are loyal on the whole and confident of our ultimate victory but we ourselves have taught them to consider the future and they will not trouble much to help us gain our victory if they do not think the future will bring them more cash, more opportunities, more importance, and more freedom from what they consider, rightly or wrongly, the domination of UAC.

In this résumé I referred to the fact that events in India had brought self-government into prominence in Nigerian minds. I have no clue to the exact date – it must have had some connection with the visit to India of Sir Stafford Cripps early in 1942 – but I remember clearly and with extraordinary vividness that some newspaper report sent as it were an electric shock throughout Lagos. (The bush shrugged its shoulders.) India was going to have complete independence. Then why not Nigeria? It had been promised them by successive Governors, but most of the people had hardly listened nor grasped the full meaning of the words. For some years, there had been an active and vocal minority of English-educated – and even more of American-educated – men who talked a great deal about imperialists and oppressors and slavery and martyrdom, which they contrasted with the freedom and power that self-government would bring, but it had all sounded rather remote and nebulous to the bulk of the people. Amongst the more advanced, there was of course a most legitimate desire to shake off the leading strings (which the journalists more dramatically called chains) and to prove their own worth, yet even with them, there did not seem any great urgency. They wanted independence, they looked forward to it in some foreseeable but still indeterminate future. Then all of a sudden, from one day to another, it almost seemed from one hour to another, they wanted it at once, the next day, that very evening.

Whether it was the pent-up longing of years, the clamour for liberty so long stifled, the cry of the patriot who has seen his land despoiled, or the unthinking, excited demand of a child for a new toy, was hard to tell.

When France re-entered the war, PERO broke up. I returned to war-battered England wondering what face Nigeria would show me if I ever saw her again.

PART VI: 1951–1955

Between Sylvia Leith-Ross's departure from Nigeria in 1943 and her return in 1951 at the age of sixty-three the country had undergone dramatic political changes, so much so that she could hardly recognize the place she so dearly loved. Self-government was not only the avowed goal of the Nigerian nationalist leaders, but it was now accepted as an objective by the colonial government. The main difference between the politicians and the administrators was the speed at which each thought this objective could realistically be achieved. It was also clear that not only would internal self-government be granted at some as yet unspecified date to Nigeria by the British Government but that eventually Nigeria would become an independent nation. A new constitution drawn up after nation-wide consultations had already been agreed. Under it the three regions into which Nigeria was now grouped – Northern, Eastern and Western – were each to have its own House of Assembly with legislative powers and its own Executive Council. These Houses of Assembly would then choose members to represent them in a central House of Representatives with its own Council of Ministers.

In the context of the rapid devolvement of political power on to Nigerians, Sylvia Leith-Ross arrived in Onitsha with a plan to establish a 'finishing school' for girls where wives and daughters of the élite could be prepared for the social responsibilities which would inevitably fall upon them with the approach of self-government.

At the time of her arrival the politicians were already making preparations to contest the elections to the Eastern Regional House of Assembly due to take place at the end of the year.

★

Has history any parallel of men working consistently and conscientiously towards an objective, the attainment of which will more than likely mean the end of their careers and life work?

'Was It Worth It?',
a BBC broadcast on the Indian
Civil Service in Burma.

The war was over. Nigeria had crossed the threshold into a new world and was hastening to take her place among the nations. The level of education rose sharply and women were taking a greater place in social life.

Still bound to Nigeria, I wanted to start a sort of 'finishing school' for girls who were likely to marry educated Africans and would be called upon to entertain 'European-fashion'. The plan had been commended on all sides and Onitsha seemed a suitable centre, yet when I came out early in 1951, Nigeria showed me the face of a stranger.

The few weeks I spent in Lagos exemplified how far both white and black had travelled since I was last there. Except for personal friends and the older officials, I recognized neither Europeans nor Africans. You met people you could not place and wondered how they had got there and what they were doing. Often they hardly seemed to know themselves, and you could not get behind their tedious superficial talk and spurious heartiness. I was asked to a cocktail party: black and white and Syrian, a visiting English journalist, and a sprinkling of young men from Chelsea in checked shirts and knotted scarves. What had they to do with the country and what had the country to do with them? (An irrelevant memory crossed my mind: Lugard, his ADC, a brown teapot and an iron tray in the Government House of 1913. . . .) That the party should be multi-racial was very right; our host and his wife set everyone talking; the guests laughed loudly and capped each other's jokes. Did we like each other any the better for all this jollity?

But Lagos was not Nigeria, and my spirits rose as I drove eastward towards Onitsha, staying with new and old friends on the way. All the same, nothing seemed quite familiar. It was as if the well-known figures and scenes were reflected in a slightly distorting mirror. Only the Niger, seen from the Asaba rest-house, flowing grandly in vast curves, was its timeless, change-less self.

It was in Onitsha, which I had known so well, that the change struck most. There was no warmth of welcome, gaiety had become almost sullenness. There were more shops, more cars, more cement-built houses, more signs of Western contact, yet I, a Westerner, felt an alien.

My personal vicissitudes during the next eight months would fill pages. No suitable house for the 'school' could be found or, when found, the owner went back on his word. An influential African on whom I had counted was no longer able to help; an African woman, leader of Onitshan society, was enthusiastic and then withdrew. It did not seem possible that this was the same Onitsha that I had known in 1936, when I had but to look at a house for the owner to say grandiloquently: 'It is yours!', when every door was open and the town accepted me without demur as a fellow citizen. The Administrative Officers were all sympathy but had no power to help since I was in Onitsha as a private individual only; the Missions did their best but to no avail. Bishop Onyeabo, faithful and wise friend of many years, murmured: 'The devil is very active just now.' An elderly nun met me on the road and took my hand. 'They do not want us now. They think they know everything. In ten years' time, we will be needed again.'

'They think they know everything' – that saying was perhaps the most comprehensive reason underlying the trying situation in which Europeans found themselves during those pre-independence days and the most comprehending assessment of the Nigerian – at least of the Eastern Nigerian – psychology of that period.

It is a period I would like to forget, since, for the first time, my faith in the black man was shaken. I had known him for so long, had held him in such affection and esteem, had desired such a brave future for him that I was all the more distressed by his present attitude, by the unfairness of his complaints, the childishness of his arguments. I do not think that any of the

white people expected to find conditions and attitudes unchanged. Education, normal mental growth, the effect of two
world wars, were bound to alter the balance, and very few still
held the illusion of the continued and unchallenged supremacy
of the white race. The old paternalism, feudalism, call it what
you will, was over and done with. We were now equals and
should have been collaborators. What saddened me was
the rejection of our goodwill, the deliberate exaggeration
of misunderstandings, the falsifying of all our words and
actions.

All this is now over and Nigerian independence has been
achieved with all the dignity and friendliness one could wish for.
Yet some obscure sense of justice makes me want to remind the
Nigerian people that a part of the praise the world has quite
rightly given them should in fairness be accorded to the white
officials who bore with them during those intervening years
with so much patience and abnegation.

How difficult those post-war years were, no one can know except those who lived through them and who tried to keep a sense
of perspective, of justice and of humour. The last became well-
nigh impossible. In the pioneer days, humour had been able to
overcome dangers and hardships, suspicion and hostility, but
how meet the daily sneers and fantastic accusations of the press,
the wild exaggerations and insinuations of the political
speeches? Sir Alan Burns was right when he wrote in his book
Colour Prejudice that the white man began by taking insults as a
joke but in the end became exasperated and unconsciously
affected in his dealings with the African. The wonder was that
any sensitive official could at that time keep a shred of liking for
the people or have any hope for our future relationship. Blame
rests heavily on Press and politicians for creating a needless
strain during this ultra-sensitive period. And all the more credit
is due to the Administrative Officer carrying on with his hum-
drum tasks, marking the site of a new market or maternity home;
encouraging the villagers to make their own roads; hearing the
conflicting claims in some intricate land case; doing his best to
make the new Local Government schemes work; dealing with
the endless financial muddles of newly established Town Councils; seeing his own status constantly diminished and his powers
whittled away; realizing that half the work he and his like had

done would be wasted and forgotten; knowing his own personal future held no security whatever.

Dr Azikiwe's party,[1] the National Council of Nigeria and the Cameroons (NCNC), affirmed it was neither Communist nor anti-Christian. This was probably true in a broad sense. As far as Christianity was concerned, the party's representatives opposed all dogma though they referred constantly to the New Testament and quoted Christ's sayings in and out of season. It was disagreeable, this bandying to and fro of God's name for political purposes. The so-called National Church of Nigeria and the Cameroons* exploited a Christ-Azikiwe comparison in the sporadic services held by its ministers and aimed at 'freeing the people from religious "imperialism"'. 'The National Church has come to stay and nothing will hinder its progress until salvation has come to the people. . . . Truth crushed to earth will rise again and the God of Africa being the true God, the God that saved Jesus when the Roman devils wanted to kill him, must be prayed to save us from those who preach hypocrisy and man's inequality.' In the local Ibo Press a series entitled 'Life of a Hero' was full of phrases such as 'Zik is a teacher showing the light to his countrymen to find the way out of the horrors of British rule'. The same article likened the sending to a school in Calabar of the young lad Azikiwe to the Hegira or the Flight into Egypt.

Fortunately the followers of the National Church were few and far between and the down-to-earth Ibo had no urge to deify their leader. One of the few relieving features of the general situation was to find that anti-European did not mean anti-Christian. Press and politicians did their best to make mischief between the Churches, but there was no antagonism among the masses, no falling off in church or mission-school attendance. Even the building of the great Anglican cathedral at Onitsha went forward, backed by the people's wish and innumerable African subscriptions. Another satisfactory feature was the absence of that widespread and violent criticism of the United Africa Company so prevalent during the war years. This was no doubt due to the Company's changed attitude. It now showed a real interest in the country and its people, promoted Africans to

*Not to be confused with the long-established and, in comparison, orthodox and respectable 'African Church'.

higher posts, made over to them much of the retail trade, and was generous in the matter of scholarships and special training courses in England.

As far as Communism was concerned, I had no opportunity of judging what place it held in men's minds. Possibly my one long conversation with a teacher represented the popular conception of what this till now unfamiliar word might mean: quite simply 'money for all'. This seemed a grand idea and the teacher was ready to become a communist at once. When the possibility of having to give up part of his yam crop to the State was put before him, he was no longer so sure. As is often the case, the Roman Catholic Mission appeared much more aware of a possible danger than the Protestant ones, but whether this apprehension had any justification, I did not know.

How far the Eastern Nigerian Press represented or influenced public opinion outside the eastern area and among the numerous Ibo settled elsewhere, I could not tell. I could only judge of what I saw and heard in Ibo-land where, striving to guess at what thoughts were passing through the black man's mind, I often found a confusion as great as was my own. The older literates and semi-literates readily accepted the idea of independence – but not quite yet. An elderly semi-literate woman whom I had known for years and who had a remarkable knack for voicing the thoughts of her fellow-women, said earnestly that some sort of Nigerian unity *had* to be built up before we left. A middle-aged lawyer, independent of mind and speech, intensely proud of his family, his people, his status in his home-town and in the law courts, asked: 'Freedom? what is this freedom they all talk about so much? *I* have always been free!' An African priest, when asked what lay behind this urge for immediate self-determination among a certain number of his people, quoted an old Irish Father with apparent agreement: 'All they really want is the education which would lead to wealth which would lead to their ultimate desire which is power. All this talk of freedom, the good of the masses and so on, means nothing.' Others readily and freely analysed the urge in much the same way. 'They want it because they think it will double their income' was a phrase, in different forms, I often heard spoken half in mockery, half in admiration. The speakers wanted independence too, of that there was no doubt,

but they had the prudence and good sense to see that they were
not yet quite ready and that all this froth and foam about chains
and yokes was just talk. They also wanted eventually to throw
off the yoke, but not because it was intolerable, simply because it
was occasionally irksome and, as growing men, they wanted to
show what they could do and to reap the full and undivided
profit of their doings. Jealousy of Ghana's approaching independence was a spur to many: what little Ghana could do, big
Nigeria should do also, not realizing that it was just Nigeria's
bigness that would make the task of running the country so
much more difficult.

Most speakers glossed over the perennial antagonism between the predominantly Muslim North and the Christianized
or animistic South, but in the South itself there were jealousies
and suspicions between ethnic groups, and though these
barriers would ultimately disappear, it was useless to pretend
they did not exist. It is true that the British were often accused of
exaggerating these differences on the principle of 'divide and
rule', yet in almost every private and non-controversial conversation some chance remark or relation of some small incident
would show what A thought of the people of B or of C, even if it
were no longer so baldly expressed as in the old phrase: 'Them
be bad country. They chop man plenty.'

Out of the welter of words, spoken or written, a conclusion
hesitatingly emerged: a small segment of the population, true
patriots in the broadest sense of the word, were whole-
heartedly, idealistically, unselfishly, enthusiastically a-fire for
independence. A larger segment was made up of forward-
looking men of law, business, or civil servants, strong personali-
ties ambitious for their country and themselves, seeing in independence the immediate opportunity to prove their country's
capacity and their own worth, confident that they 'knew everything'. Behind them came the agitators and self-seekers; a few
who hated the white man as such, or men who had a grievance,
old scores to pay off. But how tiny, though vocal, were their
numbers compared to the silent millions to whom it was doubt-
ful whether it was even known what the word 'independence'
really meant. In the widely-spreading Ibo villages, where they
wrangled busily among themselves but could not brook the idea
of being controlled by unknown and unseen Ministers at far-off

Regional Headquarters or by slick lawyers filling their own pockets, their District Officers heard again and again the cry: 'If you go, who will protect us?' A small tribe down in the creeks boldly wrote to the Governor-General: 'If this thing they call independence comes to Nigeria, *we* do not want it.'

Though independence was the chief topic, my many conversations brought other points which seemed worth recording since the voice of 'the man in the street' is seldom heard. An exceptionally intelligent and high-principled non-Ibo Education Officer gave an analysis of the changed black-white attitude which strikingly confirmed what had already been told me in Lagos in 1943. In the pre-war days, administrative and other officials who came out were sure of themselves, had traditions, lived up to high standards of conscientiousness and integrity. They were picked men and they knew it. They lived apart from the African except during work hours when it was 'Do this, do that,' and the black man, believing in the white man's superiority, did it. Probably the system was a good one as far as work was concerned, but the white man knew little of native life and cared less, except for a few individuals.

Then came the 1939 war. Hundreds of strangers came into Nigeria and, having no stake in the country and no sense of 'responsibility' as the Government people had, behaved much more easily and informally. So the Africans decided that this was the 'natural' European and the Government people were a special class. Also, as many of these Europeans – soldiers, foremen, etc – were fairly ignorant people, the Africans had for the first time the pleasure of knowing more than the white man did. Up till then, if they had queried a white man's statement, they would have been snubbed, but the war-time white man, not bothering about prestige or importance, simply and casually agreed to the correction. On the whole, these newcomers were liked; they were friendly and, the speaker repeated, more natural, more human.

But when the war was over and the white population returned more or less to normal, the African no longer knew where he was. He had seen that he could be the mental superior of the white man; why should he again be relegated to the background? The speaker did realize that some Europeans – he gave special credit to the Missions – were making efforts to bridge the gulf, but not enough. Why could we not talk to each other more, meet more often, discuss things together? He realized how unpunctual, how forgetful his people were when it came to social duties, but it was for us, the European, to make the greater effort. There was no aggressiveness in his voice but rather a sincere pleading for a better understanding, and though it was possible to find many excuses, I had to admit that we had not always done enough. All the same, this contact was neither easy to make nor to maintain. When I lived in the bush, it had been simple: we lived so close together that our daily doings were bound to mingle, but as soon as any *distance* was involved, even the short distance between the town and the European quarters, it somehow became a barrier to any intercourse less formal than the opening of a school fête or the reception of some Minister. There were also practical hindrances: our times for work, for play, for meals differed; when we thought we had given a definite invitation with time and date, it was taken as a suggestion which might or might not be carried out; we were seldom asked to African homes, and to call unasked seemed inquisitive. Though Colin Hill, then Senior District Officer, Onitsha, and his wife, most welcoming of hosts, kept open house for Africans and Europeans alike, only one young lawyer ever dropped in. I myself remember how often I had visited a house by appointment and found nobody in, sent a note and received no reply, waited at a meeting place and no one came. Small matters of little significance, yet they form the groundwork of social relations on which to build the pleasant acquaintanceship which leads to a valuable friendship. Both sides missed much and both sides, in different ways, were to blame, although ours was the heaviest share.

'Black and white do not *think* alike,' said, puzzled and depressed, a well-meaning Ibo senior clerk, full of good-will. 'I want to help but what can I do?' On another occasion the Education Officer voiced the same thought but blamed the white man for not endeavouring more earnestly to understand the black man. That the reverse was equally true would not have occurred to him nor to any of his compatriots whom I met. It had not struck them that the impending reversal of roles, when they would be masters and the white men would be servants, presented any psychological difficulty or any necessity for the

European to make a tremendous effort of adjustment. Even during this trying period, one did sometimes hear the cry: 'But we don't want all the Europeans to go!' That the Europeans might not like to stay came to them as a complete surprise.

Curiously enough, another subject which was often brought up in conversation with educated Nigerians was the Englishman's apparent and incomprehensible preference for the bush people rather than for literates and townsmen, although surely the latter approximated more closely to the European world from which he came. How could such an attitude be explained? Was it because the illiterates in the bush were more docile, more subservient, more deferential in words and gestures, and this fed his sense of importance? Was he perhaps afraid of the growing influence of the educated élite, sensing that one day they would replace him, and therefore clung to these last vestiges of his once undisputed power? I believe the truest explanation was both simple and so far from the educated African's comprehension that it was no wonder it left the questioners unconvinced. It is true that most Englishmen's immediate reaction to any query as to what type of African he liked best was often: 'Give me the man in the bush every time!' Yet, as far as Eastern Nigeria was concerned, no one could pretend that the independent-minded Ibo had ever been docile or subservient, so there must have been some other cause for this preference and I think it stemmed largely from the fact, as I have already noticed, that so many of the officials were country-born themselves and had an instinctive liking for the man who wielded a hoe, flung his net wide over twilit waters, seized bow and arrow to follow a game trail. These were people who lived in a world he liked, away from office chairs and files and four enclosing walls. As it was precisely these four walls and what they symbolized to which the literate African aspired, it was no wonder that a contrary ambition left him bewildered and almost shocked. This attitude on the part of the white man was of course already changing, yet there was many a diehard left who thought nostalgically of forest paths and sandy upland tracks, of the huddled villages of mud and thatch, of the sound of matchet on tree trunk, of women's pestles pounding in the wooden mortars. . . .

The idea of the finishing school flickered and died.[2] The old nun was right. It had been badly timed: at the moment our best meant efforts were not needed, they were out of place. Colin and Patricia Hill, staunch friends through all my troubles, asked me to come and stay with them and I was able to see at first hand the strain under which Administrative Officers were working. Colin Hill was not only worn out with overwork, he was constantly harassed by the nagging questions: Where are we going? What are we doing? How much time is still left to train these people in all the new methods of Town Councils, Urban District Councils, rates, income tax, not to speak of universal suffrage and free elections?

Differing altogether from the autocratic Northern Emirates, the five million or more Ibo had always managed their own affairs by democratic methods. But it was a democracy founded on all sorts of intricate seniorities and relationships within a given clan, on permissions, prohibitions and sanctions of which the reasons were clear to the Ibo themselves, but were the outcome of trains of thought reaching up to a dim and crowded world of spirits unknown to white man. In exchange we were trying to give them (and they clamoured to have it since they thought anything less would indicate that we still considered them as inferior to ourselves) a rigid code laid down in black and white, made for other minds and lives and conditions. Paradoxically, the frequent dissensions in, say, the Onitsha Town Council, generally started over some trivial point of English procedure. The average District Officer was not normally as interested in the ins and outs of procedure as in getting down to the practical matters on the agenda and every now and then would do something 'incorrect'. On the other hand, the members revelled in this procedure which doubtless reminded them of their own complicated observances.

Colin, Patricia and I were still partially amongst the diehards and our happiest moments were spent in long drives into the bush. The villagers under the impetus of the District Officers or of the admirable Community Development Officer were becoming ambitious and were far more ready to help themselves by their own efforts than were the townspeople. Prestige, as between one village (the widespread area of compounds, gardens, farmlands, which the Ibo called a 'town') and another was no longer satisfied by the possession of a school which usually served also as a church or vice versa. It demanded a road, with bridges, so that lorries could ply up and down between the markets; also a Maternity Home, to which the women willingly subscribed out of their own earnings; a Town Hall, for which the men voluntarily brought the mud bricks, the rafters and the 'pan' for the roof; a Rural Water Supply instead of the pools of stagnant water which were often all they had. A voluntary tax was levied on all the villagers, including the 'sons abroad', and of the latter, no matter how far away he might be nor how long he had been absent, not one would have dared to refuse to remit his due share of the cost. When, as the very peak of Progress, a rich district collected enough money to build a Post Office, Posts and Telegraphs were sadly embarrassed to know how to deal with a gift for which there was no precedent.

Nothing could have been more satisfactory than this spirit of enterprise. Nevertheless it needed a certain amount of encouragement lest it peter out, and of direction lest it squander itself in inter-village quarrels and jealousies. Often Patricia and I went with Colin to the site of some bridge a village was building, or to a difficult bit of road where culverts were needed. All the men would turn out with matchets and hoes. There would be a babel of voices, explanations, questions, excuses. The crowd would surge down to the bridge and stand, expectant, while Colin examined the abutments, climbed beneath the bridge to measure the *iroko* beams,[3] stamped on the planking. If all was well, there would be a shout of satisfaction. If not, there would be another, and still louder babel, still more explanations that it was all the fault of the Government carpenters sent to help them or, worse still, of the village on the other side of the river which had not kept its promise to share in the work. In the excitement of self-justification, the villagers would leap up and down, shake their fists, yell with fury, and Colin's white-clad figure would disappear in a surging mass of black bodies. But not for long; there would be a sudden short silence and then a roar of laughter as Colin found some well-aimed quip or called out a telling home truth, and the whole mass would troop good-humouredly down to the bridge again to see how best to repair the defect.

These were rewarding moments during which insults and sneers, the sadness of wasted effort and personal anxieties, could

be forgotten. Back from these expeditions, one could not but
ask: if we had really so burdened and exploited these people,
how was it that they seemed so little resentful, so unafraid, so
ready to talk quietly as man to man? Fortunately, at all times,
among all people, humour is never far beneath the Nigerian surface, and even extremists and confirmed nationalists could criticize themselves with engaging frankness. 'Britain is like a
mother carrying a child on her back. The child kicks its mother
and shouts: "Go faster! Go faster!" The mother tires and puts
down the child. "Now see how fast *you* can walk!" she says.'
'Nigeria is like a farmer who wants to make a very big farm. He
clears the bush in front of him so quickly that he has not time to
look back and see that the bush has grown up again behind him.'
One could not fail to recognize an eminent politician in the swift
portrait: 'He is like a dancer who bursts out of the shadows,
dances beautifully so that everybody applauds him, then retreats
to the shadows till he feels the time has come for him to rush out
again with a new dance.'[4]

I returned to Onitsha for a few months in the winter of 1954–55
to stay once more with my friends the Hills, and when they were
transferred to Tanganyika, with Bishop C. J. Patterson,[5] then
Bishop on the Niger, admirable shepherd of his many-coloured
sheep.

On the way I had stopped with an old friend in Lagos. Among
the older men there seemed a sort of hopeless pessimism as if
they had given so much of their strength to the shaping of
Nigeria that now they could only sit back and watch the result
with a tired shrug. I had read somewhere the phrase: 'The
somnambulistic march of our colonial policy'. That year and the
succeeding year, when I was once more in the Eastern Region,
had all the quality of that grey, formless period between wake-
fulness and sleep in which figures move with aimless precision
towards uncalculated destinations. A cliché which had never
come into my head before now would not leave it: 'the reins
dropped from his nerveless hands . . .' As my thoughts touched
one white official after another, the words repeated themselves
again and again. The tired hands, the loosening hold, the slipping reins, the reins that at last lay loose on the horse's neck. I

saw them constantly and with varying feelings. On the other hand my host, clear-eyed and warm-hearted, looked at the future with happier eyes; and so did the newcomers like the BBC people, several free-lance architects, British Council men and women. They were full of enthusiasm and worked hard, happily and confidently – perhaps sometimes over-confidently – with their African colleagues. These were the people who were now needed, even if they sometimes over-estimated the actual capacities of those they worked with and, misled by the quick response, the gay confidence, forgot how recently laid were the educational foundations on which such ambitious edifices were being planned.

My dear Yomi, whom I had first met during the war in 1942, was also in Lagos, now married but just the same as when, a young girl, she would come running to meet me with erratic grace and glinting eyes which reminded me so much of the young Howa of Zungeru days. She had grown into quite a remarkable woman and was one of the very few Africans I knew then who could see both the black and the white side of a question. More and more did she become my yardstick wherewith to measure the general situation and, thanks to our mutual trust, a talk with her was worth more than hours spent with 'highly-placed' officials.

On this occasion she cheerfully shattered whatever hopeful convictions I still had and was equally ready to shatter those of the broader-minded newcomers. She was also more than ready to let down her own politicians by her hilarious account of the recent Lagos Town Council elections (based on an electoral roll three years old) at which illiterate voters wandered round the polling booths looking at symbols of cocks and wrist-watches and finally dropped their votes into any box they could find. On the subject of black-white relations, she tried to comfort me. When I said I found it difficult to know what attitude to take, she replied gently: 'Don't believe what the papers say. Be natural. The African always knows a friend.' That is true: he does sense immediately with what feelings you regard him, but at that moment Nigerians were, very naturally, so full of themselves that they seemed not to stop to think whether you were friend or foe.

Yomi's husband was the Principal of a private College and at the same time an ardent and active supporter of Dr Azikiwe and his National Council for Nigeria and the Cameroons party. We argued hotly about the local Press. When I complained that we were expected to be so careful of African feelings but that they had not the slightest regard for ours, he only laughed and said we should pay no attention either to what was said or what was written. 'Everybody knows politicians exaggerate. I would not approve a deliberate lie. I would not say the Governor had said something he had not said, but I would exploit anything he did say so that he should be very careful not to make a slip.' F.A. was a man of real honesty and integrity, yet he seemed oddly irresponsible concerning such questions. And like so many of his compatriots, he gave the impression that, though he felt bound to shout with the others that the white man must be turned out, he trusted that by some subtle stroke of luck this would somehow both happen and not happen. This eat-your-cake and-have-it attitude was such a common one that it appeared to be part of the Nigerian make-up. (It was especially noticeable among the Ibo.) Of course we often have such an attitude ourselves, though I do not think to such an almost uncanny degree nor with such ease and absence of all strain. Trying to follow F.A.'s thoughts as closely as possible, I felt sure that in his mind's eye he saw an Elder Dempster mailboat moving away from the Apapa wharf, her decks crowded with white officials, jubilant Africans waving farewell, and that, at the same moment, he saw these same officials sitting hard at work at their office tables in the Nigerian Secretariat. . . . (Others beside myself have been struck by this widespread form of bifocal vision and have found how much it added to the difficulty of any realistic discussion of practical questions.)

Yomi sensed better than her husband the imponderables of the existing situation. She recognized that her people wished to be regarded and treated as adults and yet claimed patience and tolerance as if they were children. Looking back into the past, I realized how much easier it had been for us when we dealt almost entirely with 'primitive' populations for whom we seemed to have a certain gift, rather than with this nascent intelligentsia. New conditions had created a psychological tight-rope on which we were precariously balanced: one foot was liable to slip down into a resented fatherly benevolence, the other into an exaggerated confidence in the people's adulthood. Even Yomi found fault with those Europeans who sat on some mixed Committee and said: 'Well, you are all for self-government, so get on with this question yourselves,' implying that the speaker was thinking: 'Why should I bother any more?' Yomi admitted that the point of view was understandable under the circumstances but lacking in love. . . . Nevertheless, reverting to her own people, she regretted the absence among them of any real leader worthy of trust who could claim the allegiance of the whole country, and though she viewed the future with courage, it was with some apprehension.

On the subject of education, F.A. had some interesting comments regarding the impossibility of convincing parents that the favourite careers of law and medicine would soon be over-filled and that their sons had much better have a technical training. In the past, our own efforts to convince them of this had only provoked angry retorts that we wished to keep down the Africans as 'hewers of wood and drawers of water', and though the Government and Missions were now reproached for not having had the foresight to expand vocational training, they forgot the number of early efforts started on such lines which petered out for lack of pupils.

The only other educationalist I saw was a Reverend Mother I had met long ago in Calabar. She welcomed me warmly but with a sigh. She could only spare a few minutes as she was trying to deal with a whole new set of Education Department regulations and did not know which way to turn. . . . She told me there was an enormous demand for girls' education since there were now more openings for them in spheres other than teaching or nursing. Though their mothers might still be petty traders in the market, the girls themselves now aspired to whatever in feminine dress corresponded to a white collar. And as the wealth of Lagos grew, displaying itself in the crowded shops filled with luxury goods, so did the girls' desires increase. 'Examinations have ruined education; Kingsway[6] has ruined virtue' was the dictum I carried away with me.

After the whirligig of Lagos, it was comforting to reach Onitsha and to see the slow-moving Niger again. The Senior District

Officer's house stood high on the ridge above the river. The water was already very low, the great curves ringed by sand-banks dotted here and there with drawn-up canoes or the little dry-season settlements of fishermen and traders. How familiar was the scene and how reposeful in its unchangeability. As for Onitsha Town, its exuberant life spilled over in every direction. A new quarter, the 'Fegge lay-out' had been planned and already a thousand of its twelve hundred plots had been taken up. For each plot, a premium of £60 had to be put down, so at least a portion of the population had been able to find £60,000 ready cash promptly and easily. At the Bank of British West Africa[7] small boys staggered in with piles of shillings neatly arranged on wooden trays while, three deep at the counter, richly-gowned traders threw down great wads of pound-notes. The huge new market seethed with buyers and sellers of every-thing from baby powder and rolls of velvet brocade to baskets-ful of 'stink fish' and the dried monkeys' heads needed for 'medicine'. On the whole there seemed to be a better and friend-lier spirit than the year before.

No sooner had I arrived than we were all involved in a cocktail party given by a rich, jovial and highly intelligent trader at his house some sixteen miles from Onitsha, in honour of H.E. the Governor and Lady Macpherson,[8] who were then on tour in the Eastern Region. There must have been about three hundred and fifty guests, of which a third were European, packed into a small open space between the house and the road in the hot stifling darkness. It was a gay scene: a Shell d'Arcy[9] oil man had in-stalled a temporary electric light plant, and coloured lights glowed among the branches of the casuarina trees reaching over the well-swept and sanded 'yard'. Eight maidens in trim white dresses with black belts handed round the 'small chop'; eight stalwart schoolboys in blue blazers and white shorts kept order; a few police hovered on the edge. His Excellency and Lady Macpherson, together with their host and the Resident, re-ceived the local dignitaries; the guests moved around smiling and chatting with never a thought of colour bar nor a trace of Lagos self-consciousness. It might have been a Buckingham Palace garden-party in miniature – until you looked up at the balcony of our host's house crowded with naked piccins, wrinkled old women and resplendent silk-clad matrons who sat and stared. Beyond the low hedge surrounding the 'yard' pressed the lesser folk, shoulder to shoulder, round-eyed with curiosity. Every now and then, a long-distance lorry would pull up with shrieking brakes, amazed to see the coloured lights and the official cars. Whether such a gathering served any purpose was hard to tell, but at least it had been a very pleasant one, a moment's happy mingling of generous African hospitality and unstrained European response.

As for the Press and political speeches, the spate of anti-British feeling had dwindled, or rather the party papers and party leaders were so busy hurling insults at each other that they had less time to recount the misdeeds of the British. Often one read with growing anger an article full of sneers and insinuations, only to discover with relief when the last sentence was reached that it was aimed at a rival political party, not at us. Given the variety of languages in Nigeria, the most widely read papers had to be in English. How much they represented public opinion on the subject of independence (which was then hoped for in 1956) was impossible to tell.

In the meantime, all Onitsha was agog at the thought of the approaching elections to the Eastern House of Assembly. Elaborate arrangements were made by the Resident and the District Officer to ensure fair play for all those who were to contest the election. Nine candidates, including Dr Azikiwe himself, were to stand, representing three political parties. They were to address the assembled electors in the large open space known as the Stadium the day before the voting. Three days earlier a masquerade[10] – the new term for the customary Ibo 'play' – had to be driven forth so that a row of palm-leaf shelters could be erected. For a moment one wondered whether 'masquerade' was not a term more aptly descriptive of the forthcoming election with all its half-understood English trappings, than of the age-old, familiar, fully comprehended 'play'. Had I not been asked whether 'primary elections' could only be attended by children in primary schools? and would I advise a parent to send his son to this new electoral college for his further studies?

The Resident had allowed me to come with him to listen to the speeches. We, with Colin Hill acting so to speak as impresario, and a white police officer, were the only Europeans present. The crowd of potential electors filed in and sat beneath the palm shelters, literate clerks and teachers and traders, illiterate farmers from the bush – all men, the women did not get the vote till later. The nine speakers sat a little self-consciously under another shelter, exchanging jokes and handshakes in the best sporting tradition. A tall Native Authority policeman in blue uniform and red cummerbund stepped, face impassive, on to the dais and picked up a scrap of paper out of a box. Colin read out the name of the first speaker, who sprang to his feet and hurried to the dais. Only ten minutes were allowed to each speaker and five minutes for questions. The audience listened attentively. Literate or illiterate, the Ibo have a deep feeling for what they term 'oratory', sensitive to every turn of phrase, appreciative of every allusion, delighting in a well-placed proverb or aptly chosen saying. Their sudden roar of applause might not be for the content of a man's speech but for the skill with which he had ordered his words or the artistry with which he had delivered them. When the speaker returned from the dais to the shelter, the other candidates rose to their feet and slapped him on the shoulder. The proceedings had all the sportsmanlike attitudes of a game of cricket. It was not for the white men to say that only they knew how 'to play the game'.

Under the blazing African sun, the policeman held up another scrap of paper, Colin again took out his stop-watch, the speeches went on. Once, at question time, an elderly man stepped forward, a countryman by garb and gesture. Feet firmly planted on the ground, he demanded: 'You talk and talk. What are you going to *do* for my village?' There was no reply to so embarrassing a question. When Dr Azikiwe's name was called, there was a long murmur of satisfaction. From his first quiet words to the last, almost hysterical shriek, his contact with the crowd was like a fine-drawn wire, quivering at every breath.

The next day, the voting went off quietly, with victory for the NCNC. In the afternoon, a lorry driver, master of picturesque English, gave me, unasked, a rollicking account of election bribery. A self-reliant fellow earning good money, he had no time for politics himself, but he was full of admiration for those voters who had managed to pocket bribes from both sides. It was all so frank and open that you forgot how heinous, by our modern standards, was the offence.

It was neither the House of Assembly, nor elections, nor bribery that worried the Administrative Officers. It was the struggle to educate the people under their care in the use of an entirely new machinery. A whole nomenclature had to be changed; authority no longer rested in the same hands; a great mass of paper-work was expected of men who were often only semi-literate. Obviously once a country became self-governing, it would have to re-think and re-form its system of government, and the schemes laid down were probably as good as any. The trouble was, anyhow in the Eastern Region, that the Ibo was an individualist. He would be a loyal and self-sacrificing member of his own kindred, but 'the greatest good of the greatest number' meant nothing to him. And though he was far from reactionary in material ways, the natural and the supernatural, the living and the dead, were still so interwoven in the web of his life that every change of authority, every effort to link his village with another village or to alter by a single yam heap the boundaries of his village-land, involved not only himself but all his past generations, right up to his ancestral spirits under whose dominion he still lived. In addition to the difficulties created by this half-mystical attitude, the denseness of the population, sometimes more than a thousand to the square mile, increased the problem.

Local jealousies, obstinacies, narrowness of outlook were comprehensible and could have been slowly dealt with – but time pressed. 'Local Government' was the order of the day and a beginning had to be made. Unfortunately Local Government brought with it all the ponderous phraseology of England, repetitions, circumlocutions, redundant words, 'Mr' and 'Esq'. Reading the minutes of some Local Government meeting, the only phrase that had a ring of reality was often: 'The Council ended in uproar.' This was frequent for, from examples given me, that mysterious bit of paper called 'The Instrument', which established a Council, often became the symbol of a totalitarian authority superimposed on the old Ibo democracy, much sterner than anything the DOs had ever devised. The old customary seniorities had gone by the board, to be replaced by a system of votes which anyone could buy, and often putting the illiterates at the mercy of the literates.

Perhaps it is only by reading some long-forgotten file that one can judge, not only the little capacity of 'the bush' (and that meant a good two-thirds of Nigeria) to practise Local Government on modern lines, but also the patience required to mould fluid Ibo thought into cut and dried regulations composed by Rural District Councillors sitting in the prim surroundings of some English provincial town.

Yet this is a negative side to the picture: a new generation was fast growing up which would be able to deal with the letter of Local Government, if not with its spirit. The spread of education as exemplified by the multiplicity of schools was perhaps what struck me most when comparing the Onitsha of 1954 with the Onitsha I had known in 1934. It was literally phenomenal: not only, indeed not so much, in the towns as in the rural areas, not only near main roads but away in the bush where homesteads and mud and thatched villages housed a still fairly backward population. But no matter how illiterate the parents, how bound to their soil and their crops, how narrow their interests and their knowledge of the outside world, their children had to 'go school'. That the school might be good or bad, the teachers trained or untrained, was indifferent to them, was indeed not realized. A school was 'school', and so long as the child 'went school', his future was assured. If the father did not insist, then the mother did, and it was often she who scraped and saved, penny by penny, the money for the school fees.

I drove out to Nnewi to visit the Reverend Mother, African herself, in charge of a tiny community of African novices. Only twenty years before, the 'road' had been a narrow tunnel, dark between the serried palm trunks and their arching fronds. Dense as was the population, it was hidden away behind a screen of forest, a hot and silent world in which there was always a strange green dusk and dark green shadows. Now the road was wide, surfaced, glaring white. An almost unbroken succession of clearings held Mission schools, Anglican or Roman Catholic, an occasional private African-owned school, or large, angular churches. School buildings were of every period. There were still some of the old pattern, long, low, mud-walled, palm-thatched. Instead of doors, children poured out of little round openings like ants out of a disturbed ant-heap. More frequent was the new type built of cement-washed mud bricks with a corrugated-iron roof. Newer still, a resplendency of white and silver, were large cement-block buildings, painted white and roofed with bright sheets of aluminium. Decorous white-clad pupils streamed out to well-kept playing-fields. There were trimmed hibiscus hedges, gay zinnia borders. Even little mud schools had three straggling cannas and lemon grass edging, proof that they also strove for culture and that curious thing 'white man he talk about too much' called a 'love of nature'.

As an example of laudable ambition, of energy backed by self-sacrifice, of local effort readily aided by the Missions, it was admirable. One could only regret that owing to the shortage of really good teachers, the results were indifferent. The demand had, too quickly, overtaken the supply.

When, to everyone's regret, the Hills left on transfer to Tanganyika, Bishop Patterson, the Bishop on the Niger, very kindly asked me to stay at Bishopscourt. We were both much away, Bishop Patterson visiting his then enormous diocese, I trying to gather other points of view than those of Onitsha, though remaining in the same eastern area.

Friendly though individual Africans were, for the first time I found it difficult to talk to the younger people, so sure of themselves, so untouched by our own many calamities, so desirous of a future they envisaged with such assurance and were so eager to reach in the shortest possible time. It was useless to tell them that the pace was too fast. They themselves had set the pace and found us slow and undecided. They thought us either frankly stupid or darkly hiding some imperialistic intention. They could not think our changed attitude was a sign of our goodwill, of our readiness to accept the fact that now it was they who would choose their own way. Some of the older Africans even said to me: 'Were white men different in the old days? Now they say this and that and ask us to decide for them.' There was bewilderment in their voices and a touch of contempt. To tell them that we now practise the democratic way left them cold. Curiously enough, a similar question was quoted to me by a French doctor in Morocco some years ago while Morocco was still a French protectorate. He had been there since the days of Marshal

Lyautey, the first French High Commissioner, and had many Arab friends. The older men also asked: 'Are there no good families (*bonnes familles* in the sense of well-born) left in France that she sends us men who do not know how to command?' Was is possible that 'the democratic way' was not yet suitable for export? Yet in Nigeria there was no alternative. We had started to abdicate in fulfilment of our promises as trustees. There was now no going back.

The older Africans I spoke to seemed to have changing moods and, on the whole, the tone of my notes, whether recording the talks of black or of white, was pessimistic. As far as the African speakers were concerned, this may have been because it was more often the maturer man or woman whom I met. The younger, more ebullient set or the many budding politicians would doubtless have given a much more optimistic impression. It was true that even the older people had a certain complacency: it was only after a time of quiet talk that they let their apprehensions come to the surface. A well-informed Town Clerk viewed with dismay the future of Local Councils without a District Officer to guide them. He found the ordinary clerk increasingly inefficient even though higher educational standards were now required. 'Their minds are not on their work.' The speaker became very human when he recounted his exasperation with the slowness of committees and the never-ending discussion of details. He insisted that 'the intelligent people' like doctors and lawyers were the worst offenders, prolonging the sessions for hours and achieving no results beyond the splitting of hairs. These 'intelligent people' were also as unscrupulous as anyone else 'when it comes to favouring a relative or a townsman in the matter of a job!'

This short stocky man with his bright eyes and excellent command of English, seemed to embody the best of the old type with its shrewd common sense, and the best of the new with its wider outlook and greater comprehension of modern needs. There were others like him, a post-master, the manager of a small CMS bookshop, a teacher or two, a pastor, an African Assistant District Officer, a Forestry Officer, several women. I recall with pleasure their earnest faces (not put on for the benefit of the white woman) and quiet voices as they talked of their problems. On people such as these a new Nigeria could be built, but how few they were, and how little influence they had, without money or political power.

But if African thinking was confused, so was mine. I lived in too many worlds: black, white, urban, bush, Government, Mission; in too many centuries: chromium cars and the naked palm-wine tapper, the wireless set and the bow and arrow; among too many faiths: the serene Cathedral services and the juju shrine in the dark glades; among too many words: the scintillating promises of the politicians and, as taxes doubled and redoubled, the bitter remark of the villagers: 'This is what they call self-government. . . .' I visited Mission schools, hospitals, leper colonies; Port Harcourt, where the Residency still kept its spacious air of Consular days; the House of Assembly at Enugu; Aba, busy, forward-looking, aware; the Okigwi bush I had known so well, where Shell d'Arcy derricks now lifted fantastic heads above the astonished palm trees. Where lay the answer to the vast question-mark of Nigeria's future?

If I have spoken more of African reactions than of European it is because the former were the more striking and the more vocal. Yet, in the background, unregarded and in much loneliness of spirit, the white officials struggled to know what was both right and expedient for them to do. If self-government were to come in 1956, what would be their status and their future? No one in authority, either in Nigeria or at home, seemed to know anything, or to be able to give assurance or advice. Many wanted to stay, out of a real liking for the country and a desire to 'finish the job'. These men had spent the greater part of their lives in Nigeria, and though they had doubtless often bitterly complained of the climate, the people, the slowness of promotion, the many disappointments and frustrations, when it came to facing the actual possibility of never seeing Nigeria again, they found how much she meant to them, how much she had entered their lives and absorbed their interest. They had also a probably misguided idea that they were still needed. Exaggerating perhaps the value of the work they had done, it was difficult for them to believe that the country could already do without them. Once more, it was in the Provinces that the white men felt the closest ties with the land: What about that new forest reserve?

There's Umiko's market to be rebuilt. . . . What can be done about the dispensary at Osukpo? Who will care for those miles of new roads so enthusiastically built by voluntary labour,[11] so carelessly maintained? 'Who will look after the culverts?' may have been the last sad words of many an Administrative Officer.

Of course there were some who were only too glad to get out of a country they had always disliked, but it happened that most of the officials I met in Onitsha and elsewhere were in the first category, and the best types of men were those who were the most anxious. That a considerable degree of Nigerianization of the Departments should take place was most right and fair, but the thought that all Services would be controlled by African Ministers in Lagos or Enugu made them apprehensive. Ministers' records did not always show either wisdom or integrity – how could they, the white officials, make sure of keeping up the standard? how deal with instructions they could not carry out with a clear conscience? how obey an order they were convinced was unjust or unwise? I heard much talking along these lines, expressing real unhappiness. When I tried to show African friends something of the conflict that was taking place in the white men's minds, they could not imagine it, any more than they had been able to imagine that we could have been hurt by their abuse. Only two stopped for a moment to think. The face of one of them suddenly clouded: 'We will lose our good men (he was referring to an official about to decide to leave) if we do not take care.' The other, in a fit of pessimism, said: 'He would be right to leave Nigeria in the state it is in now!'

Naturally it was among the more senior men that the uncertainty of their position was most felt, both on the public and on the personal level. They had a greater realization of the country's unreadiness for the intricate work of self-government in a modern world and, from the personal point of view, had more domestic responsibilities to carry. The younger men, for example Assistant District Officers of one or two tours' standing, showed a spirited disregard for the future. They knew clearly how uncertain it was, but meant to do their best and to 'see what happened'. The older men realized acutely how difficult it would be for them to start a fresh career elsewhere and, in the meantime, living expenses were continually going up. It was difficult for the average official to save on his pay, even though his standard of living was much plainer than that of the commercial people. The European firms were doing well and their representatives were housed and furnished in a style well above that of Government servants. A memory rose up from a past as remote as 1907. Arthur L. had written from the Benue River: 'This afternoon when the sun was hottest I amused myself by comparing the methods of the Government and the Niger Company. Yesterday we met a Niger Company steel canoe manned by 12 canoemen. Their passenger was a clerk at approximately £120 a year. On the other hand, here are two Government officials, each drawing approximately £700 a year, creeping along in native dug-outs with two canoemen each. . . .' The picture had scarcely changed.

I left for home in April 1955 after a few days in Lagos. The House of Representatives was sitting. The Speaker, Sir Frederic Metcalf,[12] lent by the House of Commons where he had been Clerk to the House, embodying all dignity and all tradition, sat beneath the Lion and the Unicorn. The Northern members in swinging white or pale blue gowns, turbaned in white or gold, sat silent and detached; those from the South, correctly clad in European suits, questioned and argued with ready eloquence and dramatic gesture. What contrasts, what juxtapositions, held together by a lion and a unicorn and the still figure of the Speaker. And later, by the Queen herself in 1956, during days which for all, high and low, North and South, were days of sheer delight.

PART VII: 1956–1960

In 1956 Nigeria was firmly set on the path to full independence. The only question was when this would take place. The two southern regions were anxious for it to take place at an early date. They were both determined on obtaining self-government at the regional level as soon as possible. The northern region, however, was reluctant about being hurried into self-government because it lacked the educated cadres the two southern regions had in comparatively plentiful supply. Despite this reluctance, and the resentment it caused in the South since independence could not be achieved for the country as a whole until the North accepted self-government, there was no doubt in anybody's mind that Nigeria was soon to join the world community of independent nations. This it did on 1 October, 1960, three months after Sylvia Leith-Ross left the country as she then thought for good at the grand age of seventy-seven.

★

Vijayaraghavan nudged Krishnan's elbow. 'Frightful rotters, the British, absolutely satanic. Don't know what we should do without them. Who are we going to blame after they leave?'

Balachandra Rajan,
The Dark Dancer

Once again in England, an unexpected opportunity to spend a few months in Lagos in 1956 promised a wider outlook. I was able to rent a part of a small house in the old YWCA compound, with the Prison on one side, the General Hospital on the other, a medley of hovels and semi-European buildings behind, with Broad Street traffic in front and Government House and the Nigerian Secretariat within a few minutes' walk. I hoped that here I would surely feel the pulse of Lagos and if of Lagos, then of the entire Federation of Nigeria. I was disappointed. Once more, the pall of Lagos depression fell upon me. I could not imagine what they did in those large and ever-expanding offices, nor interpret the clatter of those innumerable typewriters, nor catch one word which had not to do with the parish pump. The Nigeria of bush and farm and forest and busy black men's towns was apparently more remote, more unthought of, than the Mountains of the Moon. And if in 1925 the sound of the grinding of the white men's axes had been loud, now the sound of the black men's was louder still.

I saw a great deal of my friend Yomi, as vital as ever but necessarily much bound up in her difficult welfare work; two or three European friends brought a touch of reality; the house of Archbishop Leo Taylor[1] was a constant refuge and his wraith-like figure in its white cassock a never-failing solace. Yet I knew I was out of touch. With a few intervals, I had watched Nigeria for nearly fifty years. Though desiring ardently the good of the people whatever shape it took, perhaps the handicap and prejudices of age prevented me from seeing any kind of good coming out of all this frenzy of busy-ness and words. Since this was a world I could not understand, it was wiser to seek one that

I could, and it was soon found in the Museum which Kenneth Murray was on the point of opening in Lagos.

I had known – and admired – Kenneth Murray since the very day he landed in Nigeria in 1925, followed the many frustrations of his career in the Education Department, and rejoiced when he was given a difficult but more congenial post as Surveyor of Antiquities. Owing to his dogged enthusiasm, the Nigerian Museum had at last been built. It contained already a very good library, but pile upon pile of periodicals, English and foreign, had still to be arranged and indexed.

It was restful to sit there, dealing with remote subjects such as the types of fishing tackle used in ancient Egypt or the patterns of cat's cradles in the Solomon Islands. I used to read on and on, marvelling at the patience, often the endurance and courage, which had gone to the collecting of seemingly indifferent details. It was with the same admiration that I had read the early Intelligence Reports to be found in Secretariats and Provincial Offices all over Nigeria. They were pushed away into pigeon-holes, their jackets torn and stained, the sparse notes in faded ink or smudged type, the sheets often only a lacework the white ants had left. At the bottom of the page was often a name I had known. I could picture the hours of labour that had gone to the collecting of each item, the patient questioning, the laborious listing of tribes and clans, the pencilled sketch-maps dotted with question marks. (Arthur L. had measured the distance to Aro Chuku by counting his footsteps till it had become an obsession. Even when home on leave, I could hear him whispering as we walked together: 'One, two, three, four . . . seventy-four . . . ninety-eight . . . *one* hundred. . . .') I knew that often the information would have been gathered at the end of a long day's work or of a wearisome march, that the report might have been written on an up-ended chop box by the light of a bush lamp, that it might not always have been accurate, yet every trivial detail served to build up a fund of knowledge, passed on and added to by each successive officer.

Perhaps nowadays no one can realize the void that confronted the early officials. Nothing was known about anything. Everything had to be found out, bit by bit, often contradiction by contradiction, from the system of land tenure or the nomination of chiefs, to the marking of cattle or the production of beeswax. It was no wonder that I at least turned the pages with respect, almost with piety. Of all the traces of the British occupation of Nigeria, these poor forgotten, almost anonymous papers, were to me the most heroic. How good it was to learn later that they were to be preserved in safety.[2]

The Nigerian Museum was duly opened and was at once thronged by enthusiastic crowds. That some of the enthusiasm was aroused by the ingenious lighting, the varied-coloured walls, the gleaming show-cases rather than by the exhibits themselves, was no matter. It was good to know that at least a portion of the country's treasures was in safe-keeping and that in time their place in the stream of the world's beauty would be recognized by the Nigerians themselves.

While I was still in Lagos, Bernard Fagg,[3] the future Director of what was now to be named the Department of Antiquities and who was to take over from Kenneth Murray on the latter's retirement, suggested that on my way home I might visit the Jos Museum of which he was the builder and the curator. Well satisfied by the success which had rewarded Kenneth Murray's incessant toil, I gladly accepted and arranged to drive up by the western route so as to see Zungeru once more, probably for the last time. It was a journey of some 850 miles, but it was as much a journey through my life as over a distance. All that I had ever seen or heard crowded into my mind. It was like looking at films which had been exposed over and over again so that on each one a layer of pictures had been formed, superimposed one on the other, mingling, dateless, one with the other. I no longer knew whether I was looking at today or at yesterday: the tarmac road in front of me dwindled to the little path I had first known, the palm-trunk bridge grew to a thing of cement and iron. Which was real? I groped in a world of visions in which what I remembered was so much more distinct than what I looked at.

My first visit was to Ibadan University College where I stayed a week, enjoying every moment of my host's society, profoundly depressed by all else; and though conscious of my ignorance of academic life and therefore of the inadequacy of my judgement, passionately critical. Had I still an ingrained suspicion of 'Education' even after this lapse of time and at this high level? I hope not. It was the air of unreality that struck me most, as if the students had no comprehension of the nature of a

University and as if the members of the staff (of course there were exceptions) had no comprehension of the nature of the African and of the world from which he had so very recently emerged – or rather was in process of emerging.

I had seen great beauty in the very modern architecture of Onitsha Cathedral. I could find none in these uneasy, incoherent buildings. In spite of size and space, they gave a 'noisy' impression: one could imagine hurrying footsteps, incessant talk, not mental activity nor purposeful concentration. The more I looked, the less could I believe that Learning inhabited these restless halls or that Wisdom garnered her spoils in these cement honeycombs. And if I had been the architect, I would have insisted on a wider space between the University College and what remained of the African bush. On one side, it came quite close, a straight dark wall on which, at dusk, I once thought I saw the reflection of a faintly mocking leer.

But this was many long years ago, when all looked raw, unfinished, and staff and students had not yet had the time either to find themselves or each other.

The road from Ibadan to Ilorin crossed the Niger by the Jebba Bridge which had replaced the train ferry of earlier days. The memory of its captain, alone with his dead mate, his canary, and his dreams of clear fountains on coral beaches, would not leave me.

Having heard of those strange bronze figures on Jebba Island,[4] I wished to see them, but I had not reckoned with my driver, a smart-looking, infinitely superior ex-policeman, unhappily named Sweetie. Sweetie had been quite satisfactory while driving in the sophisticated atmosphere of Lagos, and it was not till we reached Ibadan that I realized what a complete hypochondriac he was. From then on, our route was punctuated by diversions to the nearest doctor, hospital, clinic, dispensary. The car filled with bottles and tablets and powders. The maps were lost beneath advertisements of patent medicines. My own loads gave way to Sweetie's extra blanket, mosquito net and tins of Ovaltine. He was on a diet – could only sleep on a bed – must drink iced water. Remonstrance was in vain. Sweetie had passed a first-aid course and knew all the answers . . . .

Yet, somehow, we reached Ilorin and the modernities of the Residency. I had preferred the picturesque long low Residency of Hermon-Hodge's day to the present PWD orthodoxy, but the generous welcome was the same, stranger though I was, breaking into a busy life. Ilorin was then a political battlefield, yet when I went to visit Moreneke, my old interpreter of Education Department days, the quarter in which she lived was unchanged. White-gowned men still sat beneath the shade-trees in endless earnest conversations. Women, blue-clad, still passed by, their water pots upon their heads. Here, undisturbed, the town still slept, aloof in a red-walled sunlit hush.

Though so long absent, it was easy to fall again into Northern talk – and how gladly I found I was still looked upon as 'belonging'. Administrative Officers had retained greater power than those in the South, but many of their difficulties under the new regime were the same and their personal future as unassured. Yet they carried on conscientiously, quietly, perturbed only by the thought of the possible dangers independence might bring. They could not forget that the peoples of Nigeria had been held together in an often uneasy yet workable whole by nothing more tangible than the will of the white man working through a small body of administrators dotted here and there. They, more than anyone, knew how little cohesion there was.

Though I had made careful arrangements so as not to be a burden on anyone, I found the way had already been prepared without my knowledge. I passed from Province to Province,[5] moving bewildered yet content between past and present; meeting hospitality and friendship everywhere; sharing old memories learning new conditions; recognizing well-loved scenes – the night market at Bida with all its little oil lamps turning the heavy air into a golden canopy, the green pools of the Kaduna River lying still between the cascading rocks – and finding again at Zungeru, on the hill where the light wind rustled in the trees, the core of peace. Then on to Jos, with Sweetie still bitterly complaining of the lack of medical facilities in the Northern Region, and a week's stay in the hospitable home of Bernard and Catherine Fagg.

The Museum, stone-built with a high tree-clad hill behind it, was of great interest and I gladly accepted the proposal to return in the autumn as an unofficial voluntary helper.

I flew from Jos to Kano. Before the night plane took off for home there was just time to see *Gidan Dan Hausa* looming black in the darkness, with all its memories of 1912 and of Hanns and Isabelle Vischer. In three weeks, I had re-traced half a lifetime.

★   ★   ★

When I came out again in October 1957, my car was waiting for me in Lagos. This time I wanted to drive up to Jos by the eastern route, as the Church Missionary Society had very kindly invited me to attend the centenary celebrations of the establishment of their Niger Mission, which were to be held in Onitsha. Wary of superior and genteely neurasthenic drivers, I chose a stocky, shabby little man with two words of English and a certificate to say he was an excellent driver when not drunk. Abè drove admirably, untiring and careful, slept anywhere, ate what he could find, never grumbled and never got drunk.

When we reached Asaba on the banks of the Niger, the two o'clock ferry to Onitsha had left before its time. The next one was due to leave at four, perhaps at five. . . . Already a long train of cars and lorries waited at the top of the gradient which leads down to the beach. There was nothing to do but to take our place as quickly as possible before the queue got longer still. The sun beat down with that merciless intensity peculiar to Asaba Waterside. The smell of petrol from the lorries, the heat in the car, were intolerable. A woman beckoned me to a stool in the shade of her little stall, but I did not dare leave Abè to resist alone the temptation of the gourds of palm wine men were selling up and down the line of traffic.

We shared a banana, and stared across the Niger for a sight of the returning ferry. It was already five o'clock, and vehicles blocked the entire road. I saw a few CMS people bound for Onitsha whom I knew, and we hoped the captain of the ferry-boat would give priority to those attending the Centenary which was to open early the next morning. When at last the boat appeared, moving slowly and crab-wise against the current, and finally lurched onto the beach, the captain did indeed give us priority, but without realizing the extent of the CMS's popu-larity nor the number of the faithful. From every car and truck and bus and lorry rose the shout: 'Cente-e-nary! I be Cente-e-nary! We CMS, we go Cente-e-nary!' Higher and higher rose the cry: 'Cente-e-nary! Cente-e-nary!' as the entire line of traffic lunged forward and down the steep gradient to the beach. The captain, helpless, shrugged his shoulders. I got out, gave my loved little Peugeot and the faithful Abè a last look and turned my back.

Though the straining engines could hardly get the ferry away from the bank, not a vehicle was left behind. It could only have happened in Nigeria, I reflected, where the possible is so often bungled and the impossible flamboyantly accomplished.

The Centenary went by in great rolling waves of sound and colour. It was an extraordinary experience. Beside the Nigerian and European clergy, officials and CMS representatives from England – and in the last days, the gentle presence of the Princess Royal – there were thousand upon thousand of Africans, nearly all the women wearing the specially-woven Centenary cloth of deep brown and gold with a design of Bishop Crowther standing beneath the Aboh palm tree. By what means they had come, how they were all housed and fed, no one knew. They stood quiet and attentive, under a blazing sun, for hours on end, pressed tightly together in the big playing-field of the Dennis Memorial Grammar School. Order was kept by a handful of Scouts and Guides and two very small Cubs. During the whole week, one felt as if the Truce of God held the world silent, awed, happy and at peace.

But even the solemn Centenary had a comic ending. The Onitsha Town Council had invited the Princess Royal to a cocktail party at which all the leading members of the Onitshan community were to be present, as also the Governor-General and Lady Robertson,[6] senior officials, and all the Missions. There was no place large enough to hold such numbers except the recently-built Meat Market on the high bank above the Niger. But, hygienic though it was, the Meat Market smelt. . . . For three days, Onitsha went meatless while labourers scrubbed and scoured and poured gallons of disinfectant over slabs and paving stones. Electric lamps were criss-crossed over the terrace which overlooked the Niger. Flags were hung, palm fronds intertwined. All was ready with band and buffet when the Princess

Royal appeared upon the terrace. Presentations were taking place in seemly order when there was a slight rushing sound above their heads. The lights were dimmed and ping! a cloud of yam beetles hurled itself upon us.

Yam beetles are the size of cockchafers, dark brown, hard backed, and when crushed, die a slimy death. Usually they come like a short sharp shower, over in a minute – this time we seemed to be enveloped in an ever-thickening cloud of whirling bodies. Hoping the beetles might only be attracted by the lights, chairs were quickly set for Her Royal Highness in a half-lit corner of the terrace. At that moment I was busy chasing beetles from under the little short capes the two Roman Catholic Fathers wore over their white cassocks. When I looked round again, the Princess Royal was sitting very upright, serene and smiling, while Dr Sybil Batley, first and much loved of CMS medical missionaries, skilfully picked out the yam beetles caught in her hair.

All the way to Jos the sound of padding feet, the sonorous clang of Ibo hymns, the clear voice of Bishop Patterson, the rise and fall of half-chanted prayers filled my ears, while my eyes still saw those brown and yellow throngs, the white- or black-clad pastors, the bright robes of chiefs and the banners held high with far-off names from the Delta, the creeks, from Aboh, from Nsukka, from Benin. It was gladdening to know that all those missionaries, men and women, who had come to Nigeria for the love of God and had often died grim and lonely deaths, had not lived and died in vain.

Jos seemed a foreign country, hard and empty after the soft and teeming South. I loved the Museum, my Director and his wife, the rest-house which the Museum had built for passing visitors and in which I lived. It was delightful to be between mud walls again after the cement ('the only material which cannot be humanized') of Lagos and the Public Works Department. All the same, I was a stranger in this unknown Plateau Province which never *felt* Nigerian. I have already said that what used to be called the Bauchi Province, or more succinctly 'the tin mines', had always led a separate life. This was of course no longer so, and tin-miners had ceased to be looked upon as a race apart, men of fabulous wealth living in Oriental luxury, champagne bottle in hand – though something of the legend must have remained in my mind as I looked round distrustfully at this alien land.

Two further visits up to June 1960 were much more fruitful. I still claimed the Plateau was not Nigeria, but I could see its beauty and its interest. Important finds had been made in various parts of the country and the Museum was constantly expanding its work. Already before the end of my last visit, the Director had suggested a study of Nigeria's material cultures and had asked me to undertake the collection of pottery. This was a wide-spread craft which had received little attention. In the North it was more often in the hands of the men; in the South it was the women who were the potters. In certain centres it was the latter's full-time occupation; in other areas it was only a seasonal one carried out by individual women or small groups for local needs. Using neither wheel nor kiln nor any implement save a polishing stone, a pointed stick and a short length of braided grass, men and women created an extraordinary range of forms and decorations, often unchanged for centuries and peculiar to each of the country's many ethnic groups.

From now on, pots filled my days. Rough shelves were put up in the Museum store and were quickly stacked with every variety of pottery, often sent by enthusiastic collaborators from far afield or bought by me within a fifty- or sixty-mile radius of Jos. I got to feel at home on those wide uplands and in the rocky passes between the hills; the boulders piled fantastically one upon the other took on recognizable shapes; shallow streams splashed over stony bottoms; a wide verdant stretch, tree-dotted, might have been an alpine valley. And only on the Benue have I seen such diversities of light, from a strange translucent green in the early morning to wild unimagined fires and flames at sunset. When the sunsets dimmed, an ashen grey, desolate beyond all words, transformed the scene to the semblance of a lunar landscape.

Yet with all its attractions, the Plateau seemed a narrow world and I was glad when the Director approved of my going on a pottery-collecting tour. Remembering the variety and excel-

lence of pottery seen amongst the Ibo women during my two
visits under the Leverhulme Research scheme in 1934–37, I
suggested I might go again to their area in what was then known
as the Eastern Region. I would go through Wamba, Makurdi,
Enugu, to Onitsha and out to Aguleri, Awka and the well-
known pottery centres of Inyi and of Afikpo near the Cross
River.

At Wamba, ninety-seven miles south of Jos, I recaptured for a
moment the feel of older days. I turn to my scribbled notes:

January 17, 1959. Wamba rest-house high on a hill
pleasantly reminiscent of all the rest-houses I have known:
same slightly sagging roof and walls, same heavy iron bolts
that never fit, same little puddles on mud floor around gently
oozing water-pots, same Tilly lamp that leaks over all my
books. The DO also, happily, reminiscent of all the DOs I
have known, correct in bow-tie for dinner, nearly the old talk
and has still certain power and responsibility. Likes the
pagans he deals with, though perhaps more remote from
them, less feudal outlook than in the old days. He had no idea
what the future held for him. In the meantime, he carried
steadfastly on. There were bush fires all around in the darkness and a drum-less silence. What of the future of Nigeria?
Will she burst into vivifying flame or sink back into her
centuries-old silence? In morning, tall policeman, having
heard I liked pots, gravely brought me a series of tiny ewers.
Fulani from Yola but, surprisingly, RC and knew what word
'Museum' meant. What varied, touching, admirable con-
tributors we have.

January 19. On to Makurdi (118 m.) by execrable road.
Benue River low, yet seeming infinite; bridge magnificent. It
was near here so many years ago that I and my stern-wheeler
'live for die'. Now, in the fast-coming night, there'll be a
chain of light from shore to shore and the whistle of the train
coming up from Port Harcourt. Next day, diversion through
remote beautiful country to my driver's father-in-law, a 'big
man' with 19 wives and much naked childhood scampering
round large clearing among high forest trees. How is it possible to describe a Nigeria which leads so many different
lives?

January 20. On to Enugu (254 m.) where new, very modern Government buildings spring up overnight. My kind hosts were Army: he despairing of a country which cannot keep up its roads; she of a society which had developed no 'team spirit'. Valiantly, sensibly, friendlily, she had tried to establish a link between herself and the wives of the few Nigerian officers and NCOs, but apparently in vain. I suppose we always make the mistake of not realizing how full their own lives are with activities as varied as, but different from, ours, and how they do not quite understand, are even a little bored, by our well-meaning get-together efforts. What a difficult period this is, both for them and for us. Went up to the Officers' Mess, well-sited on high ground. Silver and trophies from Calabar days. Essence of Officers' Messes the wide world over.

Called on my old friend of Onitsha days, Father John, now the Right Reverend Bishop Anyogu. Delighted to see him, as pungent as ever. Clear-sighted as he is, is quite unperturbed by the thought of self-government now definitely planned for October 1960. 'All sorts of mistakes will be made but does a child learn to play the piano without any false notes?' When I pointed out the child might spoil the piano or others might steal it from him, he said that was a risk that had to be taken. I rather think that what has always irked him was not so much any injustice or hard rulings on our part but rather our fussings and spoon-feedings and worrying as to what was 'best for the African'. He's always been in a hurry to see his people find their own feet and direct their own future, no matter how much they got hurt in the process.

January 24. Twenty-five years ago, saw a rose-pink pot in the bush somewhere between Okigwi and Awka, imperative to find it and to see again those noble headlands as one looks east from Isuochi rest-house. Also Mary, my former guide and interpreter of Leverhulme Research days, now in charge of a small maternity home. Grown enormous but still the laughing quip and quick repartee. Pleased to see me? Hardly, her life too full to take much account of outsiders however well-known and trusted. Those of us who have wanted to understand, *we* remember *them* so vividly because through them for an unforgettable moment we touched the Africa we longed to know; while for them, not longing to touch Europe, we are but a pleasant memory, not an event of dramatic importance as in our own lives.

January 29. In Onitsha again, thanks to the never-failing hospitality of the Church Missionary Society and of Bishop Patterson. Onitsha changed, only more – much more – so. Expanding, bustling, prosperous, very much alive and, though entirely occupied by its own affairs, a certain return to old friendliness. The departing guests are already on the doorstep and time must be found to give them a courteous and even in some cases a grateful farewell. Older African friends complained: 'No one knows how corrupt Government is. There are not enough steady people like ourselves to stop the rot.' They could not explain why there was a rot, and it may have only been the older generation finding fault with the younger. Thirty-five lawyers living in thirty-five mansions. Many land cases, and customary land-tenure getting shaky now that land so valuable. Is sufficient attention given to this development? Onitsha Cathedral still growing, very beautiful interior and attendance good. Missions fear there may be drift from churches now that Secondary School parishioners better educated than elderly pastors and no longer willing to accept latter's statements as authoritative. Fortunately new young pastors are coming along who will be able to bridge the gap. Gather at last spread of Islam among the Yoruba has received attention. Curious it is so seldom mentioned. If trouble arose, where would Moslem Yoruba stand? How questions throng upon one – they always did but there was more time in which to consider them.

Residency empty, reserved as a rest-house for passing Ministers. The Resident (no longer called that but cannot remember all the new titles!) reduced to ancient bungalow, but the flag still flies.

February 5. Out to Aguleri, once abode of every form of 'juju', now much tamed and be-schooled. Called on Roman Catholic Mission standing on its high bluff. Father Delaney, he who had a 'Witchery' where women accused of witchcraft could find refuge, died last year and by his own wish lies buried at the entrance to the little church, so that perforce the faithful must pass over him. He was eighty-eight years of age and at work almost to the last. I had loved to sit with him in the whitewashed upper room overlooking the immensity of the Annam country – his own eyes travelled further, all the way to eternity – and to hear his talk. He wished Nigeria had given herself a little more time in which to grow up – it seemed only the other day that he had sat with a chief in a hut lined with human skulls – yet it might all be for the best and now there was no alternative, independence could not be delayed. He was right. My route back to Jos lay again through Enugu. Here, even much more than in the bush, the inevitability of independence for these wide-awake, ambitious, self-confident, energetic people could not be denied.

I returned to Jos well content with my trip and with a large consignment of Ibo pottery. It had been bought in crowded markets, bargained for by the roadside as a string of women passed by on their way to stream or well, their water-pots upon their heads; or, best of all, found in dark huts where two or three women potters would draw up a stool for me to sit on and go quietly on with their work of shaping, smoothing, polishing the lovely responsive clay.

It was difficult to settle down again to routine museum work but soon a kind invitation from a German Roman Catholic mission doctor and his wife enabled me to be off again. For years I had wished to make what was almost a pilgrimage to Shendam, some eighty miles south of Jos. Shendam was the very early Roman Catholic Mission station in which, when they were at Ibi, my brother and Geneviève had been so interested. There had been Alsatian Fathers in the beginning, then Irish ones. Shendam had grown into a large centre with schools and hospital, but my thoughts went back to the Alsatians, their frugal lives, their big beards, their ploughs and oxen, their understanding of the black man through their common love of the earth. When it came to the opening of schools, their English was not considered good enough and they were gradually superseded. Coming from the cool Plateau, the heat in this low-lying plain was stifling, yet neither Dr Ahrling nor the Fathers who lived at the Mission allowed fatigue and discomfort to diminish their enthusiasm or to shorten their long hours of work. It was not till the evening that I was taken to see the newly-built church which stood on the site of the very first one my brother had known over fifty years before. It was already dusk, and the white building was only a shimmer amid trees and massed frangipani of which the pink blossoms reflected the pink gleams in a darkening sky of translucent blue. The quiet was intense, well-nigh tangible. 'It is very peaceful here,' murmured my host.

Next day, renewing my quest for pots, I found by chance another scene of peace. Trusting to rumours of 'plenty pots fine too much', I drove to an elusive market by one of those dirt roads which had bridges but also notices asking you not to use the bridges during the dry season 'so as not to tire them'. There was not much pottery in the tiny market, but a renewed vision of earlier days. The town of Kwande was collecting tax, that is to say, a white-gowned *Seriki* (chief) sat on a camp-chair under a tree, a camp-table before him on which fluttered many papers held down by large stones. Round him squatted his Treasurers and Councillors with little heaps of coins and notes neatly arranged on antelope skins spread on the ground. No haste, no noise. A few murmurs of 'Peace be upon you!' or 'May your days be long!' as villagers poured their coins upon the table and received their tax receipts in exchange. The coins were handed over to one of the venerable old men, the heaps on the antelope skins grew a little larger, another entry was solemnly made in the tax register, and another villager went home with a quiet conscience for another year. Blessed simplicities.

The visit to Shendam was to be my last sight of the bush for a long time. Among the friendly people, the sunlit fields, the quiet country sounds, one forgot how near was the day of independence now to be proclaimed on 1 October, 1960. Back in Jos, I felt once more the isolation of the Plateau from the mainstream of Nigeria's life, and though there was still much to do in the Museum, especially as my return to the country was necessarily uncertain, a warm invitation from the MacRows (he was then

still Editor of that excellent review *Nigeria Magazine*) decided
me to fly down to Lagos for a week

I drove round Lagos. Each time you thought: 'How
changed!', you looked again and found: 'How little changed!' A
great deal had been done: much of the slums had been cleared;
handsome new buildings rose against the skyline. Lagos seemed
reborn into a gleaming world of dazzlingly white cement, glit-
tering chromium, plate glass and strip lighting. Then you
turned a corner and all the old Lagos was there, the pot-holed
streets, the shacks and roadside stalls, the tumble of houses of all
shapes and sizes set at all angles, the stained steps, the rickety
balconies and shuttered windows, the milling, variegated, talka-
tive crowds. The hot damp air held the odour of palm-oil, dried
fish, and the familiar yet indescribable smell of the lagoon.

It was only at Apapa, now covered with desirable residences,
that the transformation was complete. The military occupied a
large part, already looking mature and long-established in comparison to the bright blues and pinks, cupolas and loggias, of the
new commercial community homes. It is all to the good, this
spreading-out over the once useless waste of mud and sand. But
there is, or will be, another side of Apapa. Late one afternoon,
my host took me up the harbour in his outboard boat. How
lovely the harbour looked, level golden light striking the big
ships at anchor. Even the forest of cranes along the wharves on
the Apapa side had beauty. Yet behind them in their wake will
come the rows and rows of little houses, the local equivalent of
the pub at the corner, the bored youths, the discontented wives.
Not yet, but can Industry and African laughter go together?

I think of the railway being built. Labour was perhaps occasionally just a little 'forced', but it was mostly local. It was
scantily paid, but in right proportion to the cost of living. And
did not the careful Resident insist that musicians should accom-
pany each team of labourers so that they lifted and struck their
picks to the rhythm of their own drums and the little high-
pitched flutes? Then came the first Trade Union leader, straight
out from Britain. I went to a lecture he gave in Lagos. How bewildered the man was. He had been told there were Unions in
every town, yet he did not find they had much understanding of
true Trade Unionism. It was all rather disappointing. I listened,
baffled, and then realized what he thought were Trade Unions

in the British sense were the ordinary Tribal Unions to be found in each town, caring for their own members in sickness or poverty, settling disputes according to their own particular tribal custom, but having naught to do with anything so new and so delicate as Industrial Relations.

Of course large-scale industry has to come if the country is to survive. The Nigerians themselves demand it, seeing only the wealth and power it brings, not the grime, the tediousness, the confinement and continual discipline so foreign to the African. Yet perhaps he may find a different and a better way than we have, and his eyes may glint and his teeth gleam and his body sway to some soundless tune even in 'the dark Satanic mills'.

There was an Electricians' Trade Union Conference meeting in the British Council's newly-built hall. An architect friend who often talked with the members found they were well up in statistics, wages, etc, but that they had no idea of the context. They complained, for instance, that they were only paid one-third of what a British electrician gets. My friend told them that rents were higher. 'Then you can take a smaller and cheaper house,' they replied, unable to realize that there are no 'cheaper houses' below a certain minimum (which would still appear very high in their eyes).

All education has unavoidably been hampered by this lack of context and of background. Though the gap will gradually be filled, it leads at present to many misconceptions and misunderstandings, especially as the European newcomer has difficulty in believing what a vacuum can lie behind those bright, attentive faces and how slight is the framework into which are fitted so many unrelated facts. To ignore this handicap of lack of background leads to disappointment on the part of the European and, what is more serious, to injustice towards the African.

As always, it was a great pleasure to meet again my friend Yomi, though I could see little of her as she was one of the three Nigerian representatives at a symposium on Child Welfare which met for long and discursive hours. I could not help wondering whether the Nigerians themselves would not think out much sounder plans for dealing with their social problems than the most experienced and sympathetic aliens? After all, most of their tribal laws were very sensible, on the whole humane, and showing much knowledge of human nature.

Though conditions have changed, is there any reason why they should not be able to do in the new context what they did so well in the old? Yomi, much troubled by the growing number and diversity of cases requiring attention, said there must be more 'organization'. She was doubtless right, but somehow organization had a way of crystallizing into nothing more fruitful than large new offices, spacious and shiny, telephones, typewriters, no visible clients nor a secretary competent to take a message, look up a reference or forward a letter. There used to be a well-known Elder Dempster mailboat called the *Falaba*, with so much superstructure and so little bottom that she rocked in the slightest swell. Surely Nigeria will not be another *Falaba*?

Among the British officials, as among those in Onitsha and elsewhere in the Eastern Region, the future of Nigeria was endlessly discussed, with confidence, with foreboding, with anxious sympathy, with practical common sense, hardly ever with indifference. The older men were the most apprehensive, for they were the ones who had known Nigeria as an infant and found it hard to believe that adulthood had been reached so soon. It was the older men again who felt, or so it seemed to me, that they were now out of place, that Nigeria was like a bored hostess waiting for the self-invited guests to go. Why had they held on for so long? A good deal for financial reasons, no doubt – what other life would there be for them at their age with only specialized experience? Authority and the carrying of responsibility came naturally to them and would be hard to give up. The bond of a common interest with other men was precious – they often dreaded the loneliness of England after so long an absence. There were lesser attractions too, warmth and sunshine, a servant or two and always, for many, an unavowed love for the country, a childish touching love, something belonging to boyhood, to *King Solomon's Mines* and all other tales of adventure, to that strange homesickness so many of us have for a place without bricks or mortar, roads or signposts. Perhaps 'the smell of wood-smoke' are the commonplace words which best sum up that longed-for, vanished world. How often have I heard a man say: 'It's the smell of wood-smoke that gets me' or 'Do you remember the dusk coming down and the scent of burning wood?' An official who had left Nigeria fifteen years ago read one of my books. 'It brought it all back to me as if I were there – that smell of wood-smoke. . . .'

The thin haze of wood-smoke drifted away. The talk went on. The Europeans were sometimes too critical of their potential successors, not making sufficient allowance for inexperience, but this was somewhat due to the African's own complacency and self-assurance. Some said this pretended self-assurance arose from an inferiority complex. This I have always doubted. It may be true among American blacks or in South Africa but, except for a few special cases, I have never met a Nigerian who felt himself inferior to anyone. Perhaps that is one of the reasons why he is so likeable (and occasionally so infuriating). When at his best, he is so delighted with himself, so sure of his place in society, his own worth and excellence, yet always with a fundamental dignity and honest self-respect combined with an innate courtesy, which robs his attitude of all vulgarity. Though unable to bear being laughed at, he is ready to laugh at himself and at his own people and, though super-sensitive to ridicule, will heartily enjoy and share a joke he has himself made against himself. Such refreshing candour calls forth your own frankness and you can talk together with ease and pleasure, humour having made your two worlds one. But at that very moment, on the eve of such a great event as independence, the deeper feelings, the secret thoughts in men's minds, eluded either description or analysis. Every moment you were faced with new attitudes; every moment you were swung back to old modes of thought. Looking anxiously for evidence that these people, for whom so many of us cared so much, were ready for the immense responsibilities they were so ready to take up, I found no answer, and the pace at which self-government was approaching could not but alarm those whose concern for the country was greatest.

The younger people spoke with a strain of legitimate and laudable pride. 'Self-government will put us among the other nations' was a reflection made in various forms again and again. That this pride should be bound up with thoughts of free trips in luxury planes taking them to seats at tables of international conferences was but natural to these young minds. Enormous expenditure was embarked on without much thought for the morrow. There was the multiplication of posts and the lavish distribution of salaries. The public services were inefficient, justice was slow.

Regarding high matters of policy, there was no sense of proportion, so that when reading the debates of the House of Representatives, one found diplomatic relations with a foreign state
discussed on the same level (though with less heat) as the erec-
tion of a sub-post office at Itu on the Cross River. Party newspapers contained little else save vituperations between Ministers
and mutual accusations of tyranny, brutality, malice and double-
dealing. The question of the status of Ilorin and of the Middle
Belt was one full of menace.[7]

To its over-anxious friends, the future of the Federation of
Nigeria looked dark indeed. Then I remembered seeing not long
before a broken-down lorry being towed by another lorry.
Apparently no tow-rope had been available, so the drivers had
cut down a young palm tree and the palm trunk, neatly lashed
with creepers to the two lorries, had served as a tow-rope. As I
watched the two vehicles crazily but successfully rounding
corners and preparing to race down a crowded street, I was re-
assured. The country that can tow a large and heavy lorry by
means of a palm trunk and a bit of 'tie-tie' can surmount greater
difficulties than adaptation to the modern world. When I put
forward this illustration to a friend, he instantly agreed. A black
man might find ways of doing things quite different to what we
Europeans would do, and equally – perhaps more – effective.
Keeping to the metaphor of the lorry, we recalled how curious it
was that an African, given a new car with all the latest improve-
ments, might smash it up within a month yet at the same time
would unhesitatingly drive one that no European would touch.
He would haul it out of the ravine, lash it together with bamboo,
wedge the engine with a few stones, tie his shirt round the flap-
ping tyre and, lightless and brakeless, reach his destination unperturbed. 'Yes,' said my companion, 'but first he must let the
car fall into the ravine.' That was the danger. Till Western
democratic institutions, both ponderous and delicate, had fallen
down a ravine, had been pulled out and re-fashioned by the
black man's ingenuity – genius would be a better word – many
predatory hands may have been stretched out, many bad
counsels proffered. Fortunately I was not alone in thinking that
the Nigerian will follow the road he wants to, and there is no use
in white men believing they can either lead or guide him. His
future is his own.

In the meantime, the present was still with us and it was time to return to Jos and to make a last effort to establish order in the half-built pottery gallery imaginatively designed by Bernard Fagg, who was still Director. There was also to be a garden planned by the Department of Antiquities' architect, that devoted perfectionist, Z. Dmochowski. Now there was only a stretch of sand and rubble, but later it would become a delight to hundreds of visitors.

Much had to be done in the short time left to me, and the local papers became my only link with the rest of Nigeria. Their value varied greatly as did their priorities. Pages were devoted to the election of the seventeen-year-old Cameroons Beauty Queen. Her first photograph showed a charming, laughing village girl. Her second, after a series of make-up's and hair-do's, gave a common, flashy, film starlet. It was saddening to see this spread of the meretricious. Nigeria, whatever her faults, had never been vulgar. More down to earth, the Lagos *Daily Times* reported a 'Civil Service suit instituted against the Lagos Town Council by the Night Soil Removers Union.' (So the old struggle still goes on and perchance Lagos may hear again the midnight hoot of the Ghost Train as the Ghouls and their iron pails go clashing down to the creek, and the file that lay so heavily upon my brother's desk when he was Lieutenant-Governor may still be wide open.)

Then, all at once, the Press became urgent, suddenly feeling the inexorable pressure of time, continually reminding its readers that there were only so many months, so many weeks till Independence Day, listing the innumerable things that still needed doing, exhorting the public to realize the responsibilities that lay before it.

Some of the articles and letters were very good: well-expressed, to the point, and full of sound good sense, though it was often 'they' who should do this or that, seldom the writer himself. There was an article by a Lecturer in Agronomy which contained the much-needed warning: 'Development and expansion of cash crops and industries must not be allowed to prejudice food supplies.' He advocated, most rightly, more co-operatives, mechanization ('else we starve'), the provision by

Government of research workers and laboratories. It was all perfectly sensible and yet one felt that the writer, like so many others, thought in terms of the superstructure. No one bent down and picked up a hoe. I remember Bishop Onyeabo at Onitsha, already an old man, deploring the drift from the farms, his own arms full of the yams he had himself grown as an example to his people. Of course the era of the hoe will very soon come to an end, but it would be wise if the Agronomists could keep this humble tool before their eyes as a reminder of reality. Else 'Agronomy', with its flavour of textbooks and classrooms, will become like 'Hygiene', a word on a blackboard, unrelated to living.

The Lagos *Daily Times* had opened a competition for the best letter on 'Self-Government and What Does it Mean?' Over five hundred letters had been received, almost all from young people. It was reassuring to find that they realized self-government did not mean an immediate ease of life. There were even references to Sir Winston Churchill's 'blood, sweat and tears'. Hard work and honesty were oft-repeated words. 'A self-governing Nigeria will have to carry her own burdens.' 'If you are patriotic, you will not evade your fair tax, for in a self-governing Nigeria huge sums of money will be required to carry out development.' There were frequent criticisms: 'The average civil servant is more interested in his pay packet than in the contribution he could give to make the State machinery function more smoothly.' Bribery was often condemned, as well as laziness and self-seeking. It was also reassuring to feel the pride and confidence in all these young hearts: 'This new self-government will neither fail nor break down, but will make peace and harmony reign supreme in Nigeria.'

'Harmony' – that was the word that caused the older European officials so much anxiety, nor were they apparently alone in their disquiet. The Lagos *Daily Times* published an ably-written article entitled 'We Need a Common Ideology'. I quote the final sentence: 'We have seen . . . the people's struggle against a common enemy. Curiously enough there will be many who will be sorry to see him [the imperialist] go. For the presence of the imperialists and the universal desire to send them away have given us some vestige of unity. Committed to a common cause, we have forgotten our mutual antipathies and suspicions. But now that the inspiration has been removed, there is the fact that we might look around and find we have little in common.' This indeed was the cloud on the horizon.

In the meantime, away in Jos, pottery held all my attention. Binta, the Jarawa potter woman who worked for the Museum, had sent word that she was firing her pots that night (I was to fly home the next day) in the stone-breaker's yard close to the Museum. I had seen the unbaked pots standing in her hut, forty or fifty of them, lovely curving water-pots, fragile little flasks, stout homely cooking pots, and one magnificent, intricately decorated 'roof-top pot'. Some were yellow as the clay from which she made them, others had been tinted a soft red. All were formed with loving care and perfect symmetry, brought about by hand and eye alone.

Binta did not begin to stack them till dusk, and it was dark before she had finished building the fire of grass and brushwood. All her movements were sure, unhurried, in a sequence that appeared inevitable. This was not work, it was rather a collaboration between the woman and the elements.

She spoke little, for this was too serious a moment for talk. Back and forth she went, gathering the green leaves, brushwood, grass. When I was able to guess what she was doing, I helped, scrabbling in the dark, or sat still on a stone watching her. The night was very silent, with a small moon. Binta was just visible as she moved about, almost noiseless, stacking great sheaves of dry grass round the leaf-covered pots with unerring rhythmic gestures. The branches which stirred gently above my head, the stars which swung slowly above the branches moved in unison with her, and for one indescribable moment I was admitted, merged, one with Africa, the night, the warm earth, the woman and her work.

Binta went to her hut to fetch the embers wherewith to light the fire. The flames sprang up into the night with a roar, then died down to a steady deep red. Had the heat been too sudden or too great? Early next morning when the ashes had cooled, of all that patient work only nine small pots were intact. Binta was stoic though bewildered. Such a disaster had never happened to her before, yet she was sure no one had made 'bad medicine'

against her. Perhaps it was because she was unhappy in Jos. . . .
She would go back to her village among the rocky hills. . . .

She carefully dusted the ashes from off the undamaged pots
and held them out to me: 'I give them to you. Take them.'

It was the end of my Nigerian days. In three months' time, it
would be the end of British rule in the Protectorate of Nigeria
and Colony of Lagos.

30 June, 1960

POSTSCRIPT

It was not, after all, quite the end. I returned to the Jos Museum a number of times until 1969. The new section built to house the growing collection of pottery had been finished. A cool green garden where shallow tanks reflected light-leaved trees had been created. The whole had been surrounded by a mud-walled arcade with carved posts upholding the grass-thatched roof. The pots were of all kinds and from every part of the country, well over a thousand of them, smooth textures and springing forms, boldly flaring or softly curving lips, double handles on great heavy bodies. There were ornamental water-jars, gay in white and blue for a bride, or stately in burnished red-gold clay, a squat beaker all askew, tiny bowls for giving a sip of water to a child, the whole intimate home-life of Nigeria spread before one's eyes.

Seldom did echoes of a wider Nigeria reach my ears. On a visit to the South, a missionary said people were quoting again the old Hausa prophecy: 'The day will come when we will wash our horses' feet in the sea,' and looked half-fearfully, northward. Amongst some old papers, I found a cutting from the Hausa-English newspaper *Gaskiya Ta Fi Kwabo* referring to the Commission of Enquiry into the Kano Riots (May 1953) of the year before, when both Hausa and immigrant Ibo lives were lost. A sentence struck me: 'We were conquered by the white man but he did not enslave us and now those that did not conquer us seek to enslave us. . . .' There was self-justification in it; did it also contain a threat? But that sentence was written eight years ago and could mean nothing now that a united Nigeria walked happily forward to a golden future.

I was too far away to know what slowly dimmed that future, what caused the sudden sagging of that bright edifice that both black and white had been so proud of. The assassination of Sir Abubakar Tafawa Balewa, the Federal Prime Minister, in 1966 came as a personal shock;[1] the terrible Northern massacres of Ibo settlers, traders, clerks, skilled workmen, civil servants in 1967 may have had some reasons but no excuses; the civil war between 'Biafra' and the Federal Government, to those of Nigeria's friends who loved her as a whole, seemed the end.

One day, by chance, I picked up my abandoned notes and turned the last few pages. 'Yes,' said my companion, 'but first he must let the car fall into the ravine.' The shining, beautiful car Nigeria inherited in 1960 had indeed crashed into a ravine. She will surely pull it out again and, re-fashioned, re-modelled, drive it forth once more into a surer future.

S.L.-R.
1971

NOTES

1   Sir Frederick (later Lord) Lugard, GCMG, CB, DSO, PC, was born in 1858 and educated at Rossall School. He served in Afghanistan, Burma, Nyasaland and British East Africa before raising the West African Frontier Force in 1897. He was appointed High Commissioner of the Protectorate of Northern Nigeria in 1900, leaving in 1906 to become Governor of Hong Kong. In 1912 he returned to Nigeria with the task of amalgamating the Northern and Southern Protectorates, which he completed in 1914, staying on as Governor-General of Nigeria from 1914 until 1919. He died in 1945.

2   Lieutenant-Colonel (later Sir James) Willcox was Commandant of the West African Frontier Force and was appointed commander of the Ashanti Field Force sent to put down the rising of Ashanti against British rule in 1900.

3   The Aro Expedition was a major punitive expedition undertaken by the British against the Aro of Aro Chukwu who had once controlled a major part of the trade of south-eastern Nigeria. As the historian of the Protectorate of Southern Nigeria, J. C. Anene, put it, 'there were no doubts . . . in the minds of the Protectorate administrators that the one remaining obstacle to the consolidation of Imperial rule was the Aro' (J. C. Anene, 'The Southern Nigeria Protectorate and the Aro, 1900–02', *Journal of the Historical Society of Nigeria*, I, 1, 1956).

4   A Lord's lamp 'was a kerosene lamp mounted upon four legs which could be set up on a sandbank, or on a rock, or in the middle of a river – wherever one wanted it' (Sylvia Leith-Ross to Charles Allen in Charles Allen (ed.), *Tales from the Dark Continent*, London, 1979, p. 27).

5   The Church Missionary Society, commonly known as the CMS, was established in 1799 by Evangelical Anglicans. It began its work in Freetown and then with the assistance of its African converts began proselytization along the West African coast. Its first mission in Nigeria was established at Badagry in 1842, but it did not begin to penetrate the North effectively until after the British conquest, and was only permitted by the British administration to evangelize in those emirates whose rulers were willing to permit its presence.

6   A mammy chair was an enlarged bosun's chair, holding up to five people, used to convey passengers from the steamship to the boats that would carry them to shore.

7   Bida is one of the great centres of traditional crafts in Nigeria, famous for its glass beads, its exquisitely woven cloths, and patterned rush mats.

8   It was customary during colonial days for prisoners to undertake grass-cutting in the Government Reservation Area, and to carry out other chores – such as supplying water or clearing roads and pathways – for government officials.

9   Servants of Europeans in Nigeria were exclusively male and whatever their age were known as 'boys'. A servant might have an assistant well into his late teens who would be known as a 'small-boy'. Women would be employed only as nannies.

10   I have been unable to obtain information about the 'Mutton Club', but believe it to have been a co-operative venture amongst expatriate residents to purchase livestock which they then had slaughtered and divided up between themselves.

11   One of the justifications used by Lugard for the conquest of Northern Nigeria was the abolition of slavery and the slave trade. Freed slaves homes were established for

slaves released by Lugard's forces from their captors or masters but with nowhere to go.

12 A catechist was an African who had converted to Christianity and was trained to teach other Africans the basic tenets of the religion.

13 Colonel Sir Percy Girouard, KCMG, DSO, was born in 1867. He had served in the Royal Engineers in the Sudan and became Director of Railways in Egypt and South Africa. He left Northern Nigeria in 1909 to become Governor of the British East African Protectorate. He died in 1923. In an earlier version of this chapter Mrs Leith-Ross had written: 'Even then [1907], there was already talk of a possible amalgamation of Northern and Southern Nigeria and a rumour went round that Sir Percy might become Governor of both territories when Sir Walter Egerton [Governor of Southern Nigeria] retired.'

14 Sir William Wallace, KCMG, was born in 1856, served with the Royal Niger Company from 1876 and was its Agent-General when its northern territories were incorporated in 1900 into Northern Nigeria under Lugard, whose deputy he then became. For information about the British Residents in this and subsequent notes, I am indebted to Robert Heussler's *The British in Northern Nigeria*, London, 1968.

15 In the early years of the Protectorate of Northern Nigeria the only forms of transport were by human porterage and animals – donkeys, horses and, in the far North, camels.

16 Major Sir Charles Orr, KCMG, was born in 1870, educated at Bath College and Woolwich, and served in India, South Africa and China. He was Resident, Northern Nigeria, from 1903 until 1911.

17 Major A. H. Festing, CMG, DSO, was born in 1870, served in the Royal Niger Company, in the South African war, and in the Anglo-Egyptian Sudan before joining the West African Frontier Force in 1901. He was Resident, Kano, 1906–07. He was killed in action at Gallipoli in 1915.

18 M. H. de la Poer Beresford, CMG, was Revenue Officer, St Vincent, 1883; Private Secretary to the Governor of Grenada, 1886; Chief Clerk to the Governor of the Windward Islands, 1897; Assistant Resident, Nigeria, 1900; Acting Secretary to the Administration of Northern Nigeria, 1901; Secretary, 1903; Deputy High Commissioner, Northern Nigeria, 1906. He retired in 1911.

19 Hausa was already becoming the lingua franca of the Northern Protectorate and was even used by British officials.

PART II

1 Lugard was indeed in London at the time, on leave as Governor of Hong Kong. It is not clear why Mrs Leith-Ross should have had to obtain his permission as distinct from that of Sir Hesketh Bell, the then Governor of the Protectorate of Northern Nigeria.

2 The 'fort' at Ibi was built before 1900 by the Royal Niger Company. It was constructed of bricks imported from England at great cost. The bungalow was probably built at the same time (Sylvia Leith-Ross's note).

3 The Tiv are one of the larger ethnic groups in Nigeria, inhabiting what was then Muri Province and is now Benue State. In the early days they were known by the British as 'Munshi', a term the Tiv considered derogatory.

4   Captain Archibald Charles Hastings, *Nigerian Days*, London, 1925. Bryan Sharwood Smith, *But Always as Friends*, London, 1969.

5   For a detailed discussion see Robert Heussler, *The British in Northern Nigeria*, London, 1968.

6   A *malam* is a teacher or, more generally, an educated man. Nowadays *malam* is used as the Hausa equivalent of 'Mr'.

7   Maurice Delafosse, former bush administrator and colonial governor, taught African languages, customs and history at the Ecole Coloniale in Paris and had a profound effect on generations of French colonial officials. As Robert Delavignette wrote, while 'Seignobos at the Sorbonne was declaring that the blacks were mere children and had never founded nations . . . Delafosse at the *Ecole Coloniale* was teaching that they were men and in pre-colonial times had even founded empires.' See William B. Cohen, *Rulers of Empire: The French Colonial Service in Africa*, Stanford, 1971, p. 49.

8   Presumably this German official was on his way to northern Kamerun, then under German rule, by way of the Benue rather than overland from the German capital at Yaounde. Under the terms of the Berlin West Africa Act the major rivers such as the Niger and the Benue were open to international traffic and during the colonial period produce from northern Cameroun (as it became under the French) was shipped down the Benue to the Nigerian port of Burutu for shipment to Europe.

9   John Morton Fremantle was born in 1878 and educated at Eton and Hertford College, Oxford. He was Resident, Katsina, Kano, Zaria, Kabba, Bassa, Borgu, Yola, Muri, Bauchi and Nupe, 1904–24.

10 Dr Walter Miller of the Church Missionary Society established a major Anglican mission in Zaria, just outside the city walls, which still flourishes today.

11 Sir Hanns Vischer was the first Director of Education for Northern Nigeria (1912–19). Swiss by birth, he first came to Northern Nigeria as a CMS missionary. There he met Upton Ruxton, who persuaded him to change his nationality and join the British Colonial Service. This he did in 1903 and became a Political Officer in the Northern Nigerian Political Service from 1903 until 1908. He and Ruxton became lifelong friends. In 1907 he was seconded to Education, joining its staff on a permanent basis the following year. In 1912 he became the first Director of the new Education Department. He was the pioneer of Western education in the North and was affectionately known in Kano as *Dan Hausa* ('son of the Hausa'). His Hausa-style mud house – a building of great beauty – stands as his memorial today and is known as *Gidan Dan Hausa*. In 1925 he became founder Secretary-General of the International Institute of African Languages and Culture, now the International African Institute, and served in that capacity until 1945.

12 Heinrich Barth, *Travels and Discoveries in Northern and Central Africa*, London, 1857–58, 5 vols. For his description of Kano see Vol. I, pp. 510ff.

13 Katsina College was founded as a teacher-training institution in 1921. Later, as Kaduna College and subsequently Government College, Zaria (now Barewa College) it became the first secondary school in Northern Nigeria and produced the first generation of the Western-educated élite there.

PART III

1   The Cameroons, or technically the western Cameroons, were administered by
    Britain under a League of Nations mandate. During the First World War Britain
    and France occupied German Kamerun and afterwards the territory was divided
    between them, the larger eastern part going to France. The northern half of the
    section given to Britain was administered as part of Adamawa Province, but the
    southern section was given the status of a separate region in 1954, and opted to join
    with French Kamerun as the Federal Republic of Cameroun in 1960. The northern
    section became part of independent Nigeria.

2   Sir Graeme Thomson, GCMG, KCB, was born in 1875 and served in British
    Guiana, Newfoundland and Mauritius before coming to Nigeria as Chief Secretary
    to the Government in 1921. He was appointed Governor of Nigeria in 1925.

3   Sir Hugh Charles Clifford (1866–1941), GCMG, GBE, was Governor of the Gold
    Coast, 1912–19, Governor of Nigeria, 1919–25, Governor of Ceylon, 1925–7, and
    Governor of the Straits Settlements, 1927–9.

4   Sewage from the European section of Lagos used to be emptied into the Lagos
    Lagoon near the junction of the Old Customs House Street and the Marina. But
    residents of this area complained, and as a result a Sanitary Train, or rather
    Tramway, carried the sewage out to Victoria Island, from 1907–1933. Sewage,
    known as 'night-soil', was collected by men who wore masks so that they could not
    be identified. See Akin L. Mabogunje, *Urbanization in Africa*, London, 1968, p.
    258.

5   The Afro-Brazilians were descendants of slaves exported to Brazil from Nigeria
    and Dahomey who had gained their freedom and returned home. Many of them
    were literate, so, like the Sierra Leoneans, were recruited as clerks into the colonial
    service.

6   Much of the trade in Lagos and other Nigerian cities and towns was carried out by
    children, especially girls, working for their mothers or some other relatives. These
    children were to be seen in every main thoroughfare with trays of sweets, loaves of
    bread, prepared foods, sugar or biscuits.

7   Constance Larymore was the first European wife to be allowed to come out with
    her husband to Northern Nigeria, where he was Resident, in 1902. She wrote a
    charming and informative book on her experiences entitled *A Resident's Wife in
    Nigeria* (1908). See p. 14.

8   Sir Selwyn Grier, KCMG, was born in 1878 and was educated at Marlborough and
    Pembroke College, Cambridge, before becoming a barrister. He was Resident,
    Zaria and Bauchi, 1906–13, served with the Nigerian Land Regiment, 1914–17, and
    later became Director of Education for the Southern Provinces. From 1929–35
    Grier was Governor of the Windward Islands.

9   Dr Henry Carr, CBE, ISO, was exceptional in that as an African he held senior
    positions in the Nigerian government and in the 1910s became Deputy Director of
    Education. He was a friend of Lugard and became for a period Administrator of the
    Colony of Lagos.

10 Herbert Macaulay was a grandson of Bishop Samuel Ajayi Crowther, the first
    African to be appointed an Anglican bishop. Macaulay was a prominent nationalist
    and journalist, though by profession he was an engineer. He founded the Nigerian
    National Democratic Party in 1922, which until the mid-1930s was the dominant
    political party in the country. Until the 1930s Macaulay was viewed with hostility

by most British officials, but thereafter he was a frequent guest at Government House. In 1944 he founded, with Nnamdi Azikiwe, the National Council of Nigeria and the Cameroons. He died in 1946.

11 Dr Kodwo K. Aggrey (1875-1927) was a Ghanaian educator and clergyman. Shortly before he died he helped to establish Achimota College, the leading educational establishment in his country. He was famous for his dictum: 'You can play a tune of sorts on the white keys [of a piano], and you can play a tune of sorts on the black keys, but for harmony you must use both the black and the white.'

12 Isaac Oluwole, Principal of the CMS Grammar School, Lagos, was appointed Assistant Bishop of Lagos in 1893. He was considered too much 'the White Man's friend' by many of his colleagues and parishioners.

13 Sir Kitoyi Ajasa, like Henry Carr, was trusted by the British Government, and was a leading member of the Legislative Council. He was appointed as a member of the Commission of Enquiry into the Aba Women's Riots of 1929 (see Part IV).

14 King's College, Lagos, was the first government-owned secondary school in Nigeria, founded in 1909.

15 Sylvia Leith-Ross's report on 'Female Education: Ilorin', dated 30 April, 1929, is in the Rhodes House Library filed under MSS Afr.s. 1520. The aim of her appointment in Ilorin 'was to get as closely in touch as possible with Mohammedan women and girls' with the idea of 'putting forward in due course a report containing suggestions of how best Government can proceed with the education of the girls' (p. 4).

She was very pessimistic in her conclusions: '. . . after seven months of attention strained to catch the slightest indication of popular feeling, I can only say that there is just enough water to float the educational boat, but not a breath of wind to steer her by' (p. 24).

16 Hon. H. B. Hermon-Hodge was born in 1886 and educated at Winchester and Magdalen College, Oxford. He served in Bauchi, Borno, Yola, Ilorin, 1909-15, Cameroons 1914 and 1916, Resident, Ilorin, 1920-33.

17 Sir Gordon Lethem, KCMG, was born in 1886 and educated at Mill Hill and Edinburgh Univeristy. Served in Ilorin, Borno, Secretariat Kaduna, and became Resident, Sokoto, 1911-33. In 1933 he was posted to the Seychelles as Governor.

PART IV

1 Margaret Green, *Ibo Village Affairs*, London, 1947.

2 Sylvia Leith-Ross, *African Women*, London, 1939. Sylvia Leith-Ross also wrote about her experiences in Iboland in a more popular book, *African Conversation Piece*, London, 1944, which focuses particularly on her stay in Onitsha. In 1951 she published an impressionistic study of her journey through south-eastern Nigeria entitled *Beyond the Niger*.

3 Cowries, small sea shells found in the Maldive Islands, had become a widespread form of currency in Nigeria before the imposition of colonial rule. In 1900 cowries were valued at up to as many as 4,000 to the shilling.

4 *Osu* were cult slaves, with whom freeborn Ibo would not intermarry. Usually they lived in separate quarters and were regarded with a certain revulsion as well as awe.

It became an offence in 1956 to refer to a person's status as *osu*, and *osu* were guaranteed full political rights.

5   The open-fronted *mbari* house contains a panorama of daily life and life amongst the gods depicted in murals and mud-sculptures and presented as a gift to the earth goddess.

6   Dr Stewart was a government medical officer who, when travelling east of Onitsha in 1905, was killed by hostile villagers and allegedly eaten. A British punitive expedition was sent against the village.

7   British officials always found it easier to learn Hausa than the highly tonal languages of the South, principally Ibo (Igbo) and Yoruba.

8   Twin-murder was common among the Ibo and other Nigerian groups before the imposition of colonial rule, when it was made a punishable offence. Multiple births were looked on with revulsion, being considered unnatural for humans. The mother and the children were therefore cast into the 'bad bush' to die.

9   No land in any part of Nigeria could be 'alienated', that is, sold to Europeans, except under certain 'Township' regulations.

10   The Fegge lay-out in Onitsha was an area of the town laid out by the administration for the construction of private residences.

11   Sylvia Leith-Ross's house-hunting in Onitsha is described in detail in her delightful book, *African Conversation Piece*.

12   Talismans and other items with purported magical qualities that would give students success in exams were imported into Nigeria from India, but their possession was enough to get a student expelled from school, or at least earn him a good thrashing.

13   During colonial days the various ethnic groups of Nigeria – some of them, like the Ibo, Yoruba and Hausa, many millions strong – were referred to as 'tribes'. To retain one's 'tribal' identity, to be proud of one's 'traditional' culture, was considered proper by colonial officials, for many of whom the 'de-tribalized' or 'Europeanized' African was anathema. Hence Mrs Leith-Ross is at pains to defend her 'Westernized' landlord against the charge of having lost his 'tribal' identity and pride in his own culture.

14   Many missionaries openly condemned participation by their parishioners in traditional dancing, associating this with their 'pagan' religion.

PART V

1   The rest-house was a government-built house or series of huts available for the use of government officials or other European travellers. A rest-house was to be found in most medium-sized towns, some of them offering catering services. Many smaller towns and villages had a hut which was used as a rest-house by the visiting District Officer or other functionaries of the government.

2   'On seat': a common pidgin English expression for 'in his office'.

3   The practice of major expatriate firms forming combines to fix the price at which they would buy produce from the farmers had provoked a stoppage by Gold Coast cocoa farmers in 1938. This led the governments of both the Gold Coast and Nigeria, where cocoa was grown in the south-western areas, to consider alternative methods for purchasing West African produce and the subsequent formation of the Government Marketing Boards. But African suspicions of the companies continued.

PART VI

1 Dr Nnamdi Azikiwe studied in America, returning to Nigeria in 1937 by way of the then Gold Coast. He founded the *West African Pilot*. In 1944 he founded the National Council of Nigeria and the Cameroons with Herbert Macaulay and became one of the dominant figures of Nigerian nationalism. On independence he became first Governor-General, then President of Nigeria. He is still active in Nigerian politics.

2 Colin Hill has kindly supplied a note explaining Mrs Leith-Ross's project in greater detail than she does in her own memoir:

> Towards the end of 1951 when I was commencing my second tour as District Officer in Charge of the Onitsha Division (one of five administrative districts in the Onitsha province in S.E. Nigeria) a telegram arrived from the Chief Secretary in Lagos which said 'Mrs Sylvia Leith-Ross will be arriving yours shortly to establish a Finishing School for Young Ladies.' It seemed a strange proposal; why should a private person set up a Finishing School in a bustling and down-to-earth Nigerian market town? I knew that Mrs Leith-Ross had been author of a book entitled *African Women* but that was all. I told my District Clerk to open a new file, and it duly came back to me with the telegram as the first enclosure, with the proud title 'Mrs Leigh-Ross – Fishing School for Young Ladies'!!
>
> Alas, within days a second telegram followed to the effect that Mrs Leith-Ross had fallen on the steps of the Bank of British West Africa in Lagos and was returning to Europe. I supposed this might be the last I should hear of her.
>
> But I was wrong. Three months later, another telegram appeared (the telegraph offered the most efficient means of communication in those days); Mrs Leith-Ross was back in Lagos and would be shortly arriving in Onitsha. My wife and I invited her to stay with us until she could make her own arrangements, and we began to understand what it was all about.
>
> Nigeria at this time was beginning to throb with talk of one thing – independence. It was not a question of 'if' but 'when' would it be granted or wrested from HMG? Mrs Leith-Ross's personal connection with and love for Nigeria already extended nearly fifty years. She saw how fast things were moving and how unready – at least in some respects – Nigerians were to assume the responsibilities which would accompany the freedom they were demanding. In particular she was deeply concerned that the wives of the up-and-coming new leaders had received so much less education than their husbands and lacked the social skills which would soon be required of them. Onitsha, a town of 80,000 people, was the home place of one of Nigeria's leading nationalist politicians, Dr Azikiwe, later to become the first African Governor-General and then President of an independent Nigeria. But more than this, amongst its community were many doctors and lawyers, teachers and men of commerce, whose education, training and ability had already identified them as likely leaders of a new Nigeria. It was entirely typical of Mrs Leith-Ross that she not only perceived the problem but resolved that, as no one else would do anything about it, she would.
>
> Mrs Leith-Ross got to work at once. Soon she rented a house in which to live and hold her school – a square bungalow dominated by large mango trees, off

the Owerri Road about half a mile from the famous Dennis Memorial Grammar School. She hired a car and a driver – very polite but not very skilled at driving – to make herself mobile. A prospectus was drafted and contact made with the young women to whom the scheme was directed. A fee was charged for enrolment in the school, partly as a financial contribution but mainly to show that what was being offered was something worth paying for. Various European wives were enlisted to come and help.

All did not go as planned. Various young Nigerian women applied to join, but few had the connections and positions hoped for. However, the school was launched and ran for about four months. One student, being shown the correct way of laying a table, remarked 'It is very interesting, but you see we only have one spoon and fork at home.' Mrs Leith-Ross's hope that, once in operation, others would seek to take advantage of it was sadly not fulfilled. The young wives of the élite could not bring themselves to join or could not be persuaded that they needed to.

Mrs Leith-Ross realized there was no point in continuing. She had paid for the whole enterprise herself and it had already cost her more than she had bargained for. She could not help people who did not appreciate what they were being offered.

We suggested she should stay with us until she had decided what to do. To our delight and privilege, she remained with us three months – till the end of my tour in fact – and on our departure, she accepted an invitiation to take up residence with Bishop Patterson, the Bishop of the CMS Diocese on the Niger. Although Mrs Leith-Ross failed to achieve what she had set out to do, her stay in Onitsha was a great joy to many who met her, not least to Bishop Patterson and to us.

3   The *iroko* tree is a West African tree valued for the quality of its wood by Africans for carving statues and by Europeans for export for furniture-making.

4   Mrs Leith-Ross kept clippings from the local newspapers with reports of particularly dramatic or telling political incidents. A packet of these is to be found in the box of her documents deposited in the Rhodes House Library, Oxford.

5   The Rt. Rev. Cecil John Patterson, CMG, CBE, was born in 1908 and educated at St Paul's and St Catharine's College, Cambridge. He went to Nigeria as a missionary in 1934, becoming Assistant Bishop on the Niger in 1942 and Bishop on the Niger in 1945. From 1961–9 he was Archbishop of West Africa.

6   Kingsway, owned by the United Africa Company, was the largest department store in Lagos.

7   The Bank of British West Africa is now the First Bank of Nigeria, having in the interim been renamed the Standard Bank of Nigeria.

8   Sir John Macpherson, GCMG, was born in 1898 and educated at Watson's College and Edinburgh University. He served in the Malayan Civil Service from 1921–7, before becoming Principal Assistant Secretary, Nigeria, in 1937. He was Governor of Nigeria from 1948–54 and Governor-General, 1954–5. He died in 1971.

9   Shell D'Arcy Oil was the company responsible for carrying out the original exploration for mineral oil in Nigeria.

10   The masquerade correctly refers to a total performance by masked dancers, but in more recent years it has come to be used in Nigeria to refer to an individual masked dancer.

11   Voluntary or communal labour was a traditional way of accomplishing a community project such as clearing a path. It was harnessed among the Ibos during

the 1950s very effectively to undertake development projects such as building bridges, roads and community centres.

12 Sir Frederic William Metcalf, KCB, was born in 1886 and educated at Wellington College and Sydney Sussex College, Cambridge. He was Clerk of the House of Commons from 1948 until 1954, and Speaker of the House of Representatives, Nigeria, from 1955–60.

PART VII

1 Archbishop Leo Hall Taylor was born in 1889 and educated at African missions and National University, Cork. Ordained in 1914, he became Principal of St Gregory's College, Lagos, in 1928, Vicar Apostolic of Western Nigeria in 1934, and Vicar Apostolic of Lagos in 1937. From 1950 until his death in 1965 he was Roman Catholic Archbishop of Lagos.

2 The National Archives at Ibadan, to which Sylvia Leith-Ross alludes, were set up in 1954 on the initiative of Professor K. O. Dike, Professor of History at University College, Ibadan, and later its Principal and Vice-Chancellor when it attained full university status in 1962. Regional archives were also established in Kaduna and Enugu.

3 Bernard Evelyn Buller Fagg, MBE, MA, FSA, FMA, was born in 1915 and educated at Dulwich College and Downing College, Cambridge. He served in the Nigerian Administrative Service from 1939–47, and in the Department of Antiquities from 1947–64, becoming its Director in 1957. From 1964–75 he was curator of the Pitt-Rivers Museum, Oxford.

4 The Tada bronzes are an important group of bronzes in Nupe villages on the southern bank of the Niger near Jebba. They are named after the village of Tada which possesses the most beautiful of these bronzes, the famous seated figure.

5 At that time Nigeria was still divided into Provinces, each still under a British Resident, though this title was changed in the South in the years immediately preceding independence.

6 Sir James Robertson, KT, GCMG, GCVO, KBE, was born in 1899 and educated at Merchiston College and Balliol College, Oxford. He entered the Sudan Political Service in 1922 and was Civil Secretary, Sudan Government, 1945–53. From 1955–60 he was Governor-General of Nigeria, becoming the first Governor-General of the independent Federation of Nigeria in 1960. In 1961 he became President of the Britain-Nigeria Association.

7 On the eve of independence Nigeria consisted of three large regions – the Northern, Eastern and Western Regions. In all three other regions minorities were agitating for their own states. In particular, the predominantly Christian Middle Belt of the Northern Region wished to separate from what was chiefly a Muslim region. Ilorin, although one of the emirates of the Sokoto Caliphate, was predominantly Yoruba, and in both Ilorin and the largely Yoruba province of Kabba there was agitation to be transferred for political and administrative purposes to the Yoruba-speaking Western Region, where in turn the non-Yoruba speaking minorities were agitating for the creation of a Mid-West state.

POSTSCRIPT

1 Sir Abubakar Tafawa Balewa, PC, KBE, was educated at Katsina Higher College and the Institute of Education, London University. He held various educational posts from 1933 until his appointment to the Council of Ministers established in 1951. In 1949 he was co-founder of what was to become the Northern People's Congress; in 1951 he was appointed Minister of Transport. From 1957–60 he was Prime Minister and Minister of Finance, and in 1960 Prime Minister and Minister of Foreign Affairs. He was assassinated in January 1966.

MAPS

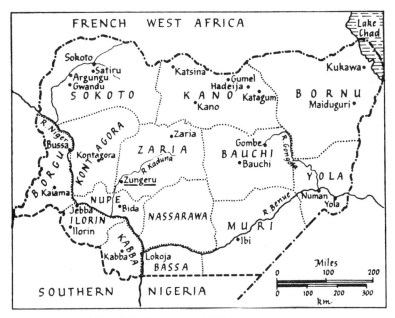

1   Northern Nigeria's Provinces, 1907
(From Michael Crowder, *Revolt in Bussa*, Faber & Faber, 1973)

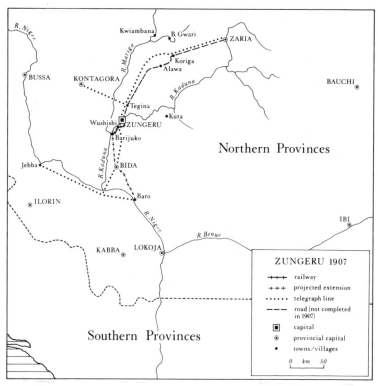

2 Zungeru, 1907

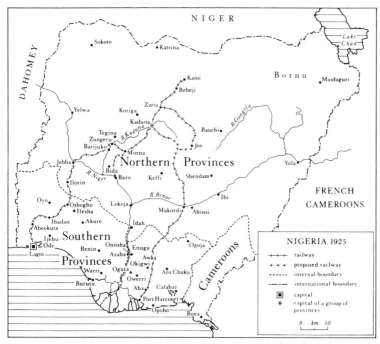

3 Nigeria, 1925

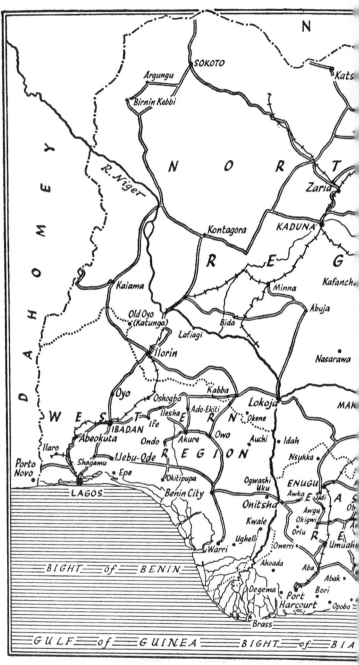

4 Nigeria, 1960
(From Michael Crowder, *The Story of Nigeria*, Faber & Faber, 1962)

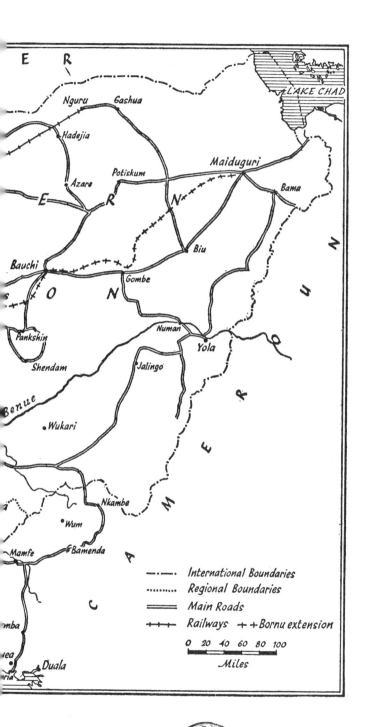

E   R

Nguru   Gashua

LAKE CHAD

Hadejia

Potiskum   Maiduguri

Azare

E   R   N   Bama

Biu

Bauchi

Gombe

O   N

Numan

Pankshin   Yola

Shendam   Jalingo

Benue   R

Wukari   E

M

Nkambe

Wum   E

Mamfe   Bamenda   A

mba   C

ea

Duala

ria

International Boundaries
Regional Boundaries
Main Roads
Railways ++ Bornu extension

0   20 40 60 80 100

Miles